HUMN
Tri
Std

EQUALITY, FREEDOM, AND RELIGION

EQUALITY, FREEDOM, AND RELIGION

ROGER TRIGG

OXFORD
UNIVERSITY PRESS

OXFORD

UNIVERSITY PRESS

Great Clarendon Street, Oxford OX2 6DP

Oxford University Press is a department of the University of Oxford.
It furthers the University's objective of excellence in research, scholarship,
and education by publishing worldwide in

Oxford New York

Auckland Cape Town Dar es Salaam Hong Kong Karachi
Kuala Lumpur Madrid Melbourne Mexico City Nairobi
New Delhi Shanghai Taipei Toronto

With offices in

Argentina Austria Brazil Chile Czech Republic France Greece
Guatemala Hungary Italy Japan Poland Portugal Singapore
South Korea Switzerland Thailand Turkey Ukraine Vietnam

Oxford is a registered trade mark of Oxford University Press
in the UK and in certain other countries

Published in the United States
by Oxford University Press Inc., New York

British Library Cataloguing in Publication Data
Data available

Library of Congress Cataloging in Publication Data
Data available

Typeset by SPI Publisher Services, Pondicherry, India
Printed in Great Britain on acid-free paper by
MPG Books Group, Bodmin and King's Lynn

ISBN 978-0-19-957685-2

1 3 5 7 9 10 8 6 4 2

For Anna, Nicholas, and Lydia

Contents

Preface

This book follows my *Religion in Public Life: Must Faith be Privatized?* (Oxford University Press, 2007). In that, I wrote about how far the total neutrality of the state to religion is possible, or desirable. I have more recently written about religious freedom in the United Kingdom in a report for the Theos Think Tank in London called *Free to Believe? Religious Freedom in a Liberal Society* (2010). The present book deals, on a much broader canvas, with how the competing demands of freedom and equality affect religious belief in both Europe and North America.

My thanks must go to many, but I must pick out Dr Justin Barrett and my other colleagues in the interdisciplinary Oxford project on the cognitive science of religion, which was for three years funded by the John Templeton Foundation. I must also mention those with whom I have set up the Centre for the Study of Religion in Public Life in Kellogg College, Oxford. As well as working on the implications of religious diversity in Europe, we are collaborating on the subject of international religious freedom with the Berkley Center for Religion, Peace and World Affairs in Georgetown University, Washington DC. The ideas discussed in this book have a relevance and resonance beyond Britain, and indeed Europe.

Above all, I am grateful to my wife, Julia, my daughter, Dr Alison Teply, and my son-in-law, Robert Teply, all of whom have helped me. I owe a special debt of gratitude to the John Templeton Foundation, which gave me a personal research grant to assist in the writing of this book, and to the Master and Fellows of St Cross College, Oxford, which generously received me as a Visiting Fellow.

Roger Trigg

Introduction

Is religious freedom a right?

The tug between the demands of equality and those of freedom goes to the heart of modern life.[1] Many find deep, and growing, inequalities in modern society unjust. If all are of equal worth, is it right that some cannot afford proper health care, and could even die prematurely? Economic inequalities in society, it is alleged, lead to great disparity in standards of heath, and even normal life expectancy, in different areas of the same city. Similar complaints arise about education. Some may seem trapped in a disadvantaged area, reflected in poor local schools, while others can buy for their children the very best education. Moreover, just growing up in some homes, where education is valued, and children encouraged, can give a lifetime advantage. What can be done to create equality of opportunity so that some are not born with advantages that others can never have access to? Yet, whatever the perceived injustices, the problem is that curing them inevitably involves a growth in the power of the state, and a restriction on individual freedom. It may merely be through taxation. Some, though, want to pass coercive laws to prevent unfair advantages, perhaps banning all private education. The end of that road could be a totalitarian state, and the excesses of Communism. Individual freedom may produce, or reinforce, inequalities, but the determined attempt by a state to achieve greater equality can undermine liberty. This is the very stuff of much modern political argument. The removal of the disadvantage of some can restrict the freedom of others.

These arguments arise not just about economic matters, but in arguments about how far people's most basic beliefs and commitments must be respected, and whether all beliefs should receive equal respect.

Should people have equal freedom to manifest their most basic commitments in their lives? Does that mean that perceived privilege be
attacked, and disadvantage aided, in the name of equality? The state
may have to be prepared to use the coercion of the law in the name of
the common good to control beliefs that may be regarded as harmful.
We then have to consider whether the beliefs that are most important
to individuals should be respected and even protected, in the name of
freedom. Yet, if those beliefs challenge some basic assumptions about
equality, should that disqualify them from having any privileged position? This changes the question from policy issues to more fundamental philosophical questions such as what our fundamental beliefs in
equality rest on. How is it that we now believe in Western democracies
in the equality of all, when many in the contemporary world still do
not? It may be a constituent belief of democracy, but what justifies it?
Jeremy Waldron, Professor of Social and Political Theory at Oxford,
distinguishes between 'equality as a policy aim, and equality as a background commitment that underlies many different policy questions'.[2]
It is all too easy to accept that equality is a 'good thing' without stopping to question what supports that belief.

Why does religious freedom matter, if other freedoms, such as freedom of conscience and of assembly, are adequately protected? This
may depend on how far we think religion itself matters, and how religion is to be defined. The First Amendment of the United States Constitution, in the Bill of Rights, makes the 'free exercise of religion' its
priority, along with a prohibition on the federal establishment of religion. It is listed before rights of freedom of speech, and of the press, of
free assembly, and of the right to petition the government for redress
of grievances. Many believe that this order of rights is no accident.
James Madison, one of the prime moving forces behind the Bill of
Rights, was in no doubt, because of his experience of Anglican Establishment in Virginia, that religious freedom was pivotal for all democratic freedoms.[3]

This is in contrast to the European Convention on Human Rights.
It is only in Article 9 that we reach freedom of religion, and there, in
language echoing the United Nations Declaration of Human Rights,
we read: 'Everyone has the right to freedom of thought, conscience and
religion; this right includes freedom to change his religion or belief,
and freedom, either alone or in community with others, and in public
and private, to manifest his religion or belief, in worship, teaching,

practice and observance.' A second clause then spells out limitations on the manifestation of beliefs, 'such as are prescribed by law and are necessary in a democratic society in the interests of public safety, for the protection of public order, health or morals, or for the protection of the rights and freedoms of others.'

The contrast between the unqualified right to hold religious beliefs and the carefully defined scope for limitations on religious practice is striking. If we compare this with the US Constitution, it is significant that 'religion' has been widened in an indeterminate way to include 'religion or belief'. The reference to the need for the protection of 'the rights and freedoms of others' is also important, as this immediately raises the question of how different rights and freedoms can be weighed against each other. All this is important, as the European Court of Human Rights has jurisdiction, in applying the Convention, over the countries belonging to the Council of Europe, not just the European Union, and deals with cases from countries such as Russia and Turkey. Furthermore, from 1998, the people of the United Kingdom were given direct access in their own courts to the rights of the Convention. The effects of this are still being played out, and are becoming more noticeable with the establishment of the United Kingdom Supreme Court in 2009. Suddenly, a written constitutional document, as interpreted by the courts, has become important, in contrast with the practice of the common law, as it has developed over many centuries. The language of rights has become a more familiar part of jurisprudence in Britain because of these developments.

The question has to be faced of how important the right to freedom of religion is compared with other rights and freedoms. The age-old tug between freedom and equality reappears in a new guise. Liberal philosophers are fond of talking of people being 'free and equal', or referring to 'equal liberty'. Both are crucial for the idea of democracy. Any democratic state must treat its citizens equally, so that it cannot deem some more important than others, more worthy of respect, or having greater dignity. The law can have no favourites, and must be impartially administered. In a democracy, the rule of law is paramount, and the justice it conveys embodies the idea of equal treatment.

We may fully believe that everyone is of equal worth, but for that reason see the possibility of treating different people differently according to circumstance. Even in the administration of justice in the courts, genuine justice might consist not in automatically handing out identical sentences for similar offences but in being guided by the facts of a case. Acknowledgment of equality need not imply uniform treatment. How far should the courts, or even perhaps the legislature (parliament, congress or whatever), be willing to make allowances when confronted with religious conviction? Should there be a deliberate attempt to accommodate such beliefs? The idea of reasonable accommodation—for instance, for the needs of disabled people—is often accepted in some areas of British law. Things become much more controversial when it appears that religious beliefs, or religious people, are obtaining privileges.

The clash with equality

In recent years, considerations of equality have come into conflict with religious beliefs of various kinds. Once we allow different treatment of different groups, that seems to mean discriminating between the groups. Yet, in a democracy, if all are equal, how can some be given more attention than others? In moral arguments, the mere accusation of 'discrimination' is well calculated to bring the argument to a halt. Discrimination in favour of religious views will seem as unacceptable as discriminating against some other group. Yet, although 'discrimination' has become a powerful label for unacceptable behaviour, it is worth remembering that every rational judgement, and indeed every moral judgement, involves discriminating between relevant and irrelevant factors.

The drive to equality has at times led people to believe that any judgement on the part of the state must never imply that some views are preferable to others. All beliefs must be viewed equally. Any other position involves unfair discrimination. Citizens, it seems, are not being treated equally if their views are not being affirmed by the state, or if some are singled out for special attention. They are not being treated with respect. Their intrinsic human dignity is being questioned. Their human rights are being undermined.

Yet, although equality can seem to mandate the neutrality of the state, the fact of state neutrality is an impossibility.[4] In the context of religious freedom, no state can abdicate all responsibility to the extent of refusing to make judgements about the character of any religious belief. As the European Convention on Human Rights itself makes clear, a state has to decide when such freedom has to be restrained. Just because human sacrifice is religiously motivated does not make it socially acceptable.

Even the idea of neutrality towards religion is unclear, as it is bound to be infected by the general fuzziness of the concept of religion. When, for instance, is a moral position also a religious one? A judgement in favour of equality appears to be a quintessentially moral position, but may itself be based on religious belief.

The demand for state neutrality can lead to the view that there is no place for religion of any kind in the public sphere. The state can then be even-handed precisely because it ignores them all equally. This is, in the minds of some, what a secular state should by definition do. Yet secularity, and neutrality can come in many guises. The secularism of *la laïcité* in France is different from the secularism of Muslim Turkey, and both are different from the separation of church and state much vaunted in the United States, but significantly not mentioned explicitly in the Constitution.[5] Secularism is never neutral, but always takes a view about the proper place of religion.

To revert to the European Convention on Human Rights, part of the absolute right granted by the first clause about religious freedom is precisely to have freedom to manifest religion 'either alone or in community with others and in public or private'. This echoes the words of Article 18 of the UN Declaration. Human rights documents themselves, therefore, do not support the idea of religion as something that from a governmental point of view should be out of sight and out of mind. Human rights are in the public sphere. The issue of religious freedom is too, and so must religion itself be.

Particular issues concerning the clash between freedom and equality come over issues of equality between the sexes, and equality between people of different sexual orientation. In both areas, contemporary attitudes arising in liberal, democratic societies are liable to clash with more traditional views, often linked closely with religious views. They may often have a wider rationale than the religious. Issues concerning the treatment of women can be linked with deep cultural attitudes, which are not essential for religion. An obvious example concerns female dress. Some Muslims demand a full-face veil for women, and others different forms of covering, including a simple headscarf. Yet others do not see the need for special dress at all. To a lesser degree, similar customs can be observed in some parts of Christianity, with some sects demanding head coverings for women.

The ensuing battles can easily be portrayed as a battle between human rights and religion, with rights being on the side of a perceived emancipation of women. Yet, at times, this may appear simply as an unwarranted intrusion into others' ways of life, and it may be seen by non-Westerners as imperialist. The clash between individual rights and those of a community can appear stark. Indeed, the ideology of rights can find it hard to find its way through the demands of equal rights for both sexes, and the right of cultures, perhaps especially minority cultures, to follow their own traditions. Even liberal thinkers can find this difficult to resolve.

A similar problem occurs for religion. The rhetoric of individual rights, and equality between individuals, can sit uncomfortably with a wish on the part of religions to abide by the traditions of a community. Should a Western state be prepared to challenge religious doctrine, so that women have to be admitted into the Roman Catholic priesthood? What about female bishops in the Church of England, about whom there has been prolonged controversy? Current practice is to recognize that religious institutions like the Catholic Church have a right to order their own affairs according to their own collective beliefs. However, there has also been an issue within churches, as to how far objectors should be able to continue within a church, without signing up to the changes. Could room be found within the Church of England for those who still cannot accept a woman bishop? This question is a microcosm of a much wider question. Can dissent be still allowed and contained within a wider community holding different standards? When states introduce new legislation, whether about women, homosexuals, or whoever, and some object to this, can they allow exceptions on religious grounds to the operation of the law? This is a question that can be applied about both religious institutions and individuals, and the law courts in many countries are getting caught up in litigation on precisely these points. At the same time, many may query why a religious conscience should be given priority over other forms of conscientious objection.

Some feel that, when questions of basic human dignity are at stake, there can be no room for exceptions or special accommodation. If it is collectively felt in a democratic country that women ought to be treated equally in all respects with men, some will see it as unprincipled to compromise with those who want to treat them in some way as second-class citizens. The law, it will be said, is the law, and must apply to all impartially. There cannot be one law for one group and another for another. We would not allow racial discrimination, the argument goes, so why should we tolerate other forms of discrimination? The shadow of Islamic *sharia* law falls on the discussion. If the law quite properly decrees equality between the sexes, how can religious groups claim exemptions so as to treat women, particularly in family matters such as divorce, in what is regarded as a flagrantly unjust way? The law should not make accommodation for injustice, it will be said. Further, the very idea that society can be split up into different groups abiding by different legal standards challenges the unity and cohesion of a country. So the arguments will go, and they can be very persuasive.

Democracy and dissent

Must individuals, and groups, always be coerced to act against their consciences, if that is the democratic decision of a country? Put like this, it becomes apparent that the very ideal of personal freedom must at times be at stake. Democracy is itself built on the free judgements of its members and would not be necessary if everyone always agreed. It is a system not just for making decisions, but for containing, and even respecting, disagreement. Without the possibility, and the fact of disagreement, there can be no political freedom. There can be no choice between alternative views. Democracy needs the free expression of the conscience of all its members, even when they pose an uncomfortable challenge.

The idea of democracy includes both the reality of dissent, and the need for equal respect of all its citizens. What happens when the imperative to respect one group appears to preclude respecting another? A prohibition of discrimination on grounds of sexual orientation often collides with deeply held moral views about homosexual practices, which can be grounded in religion. Many Christians, Muslims, and others cannot accept that homosexual relationships are morally on a par with heterosexual ones. These arguments are often portrayed as being between religion and a conception of human rights, although it is possible to have a rational discussion about the morality of homosexuality without depending on any religious assumptions. Whatever the status of people's objections, however, the question remains. Should they be accommodated in some way, so as not to be forced to act against their conscience?

These questions come up in many contexts. The basic argument for not accommodating those who object to homosexuality comes from basic ideas of human dignity and equality. When religion is pitted against rights, religion is often sidelined. The argument is well summed up by one Canadian professor of law, who says: 'If gay or lesbian sexual orientation is...felt by the individual to be part of his or her personal identity, so that failure to affirm its equal worth (in relation to hetero-sexuality) is experienced as denial of respect, or exclusion from full community membership, then affirmation is a matter of justice.'[6]

The writer applies this in the context of education within state schools, advocating 'affirmation' of homosexuality in that context. This brings him to the conclusion that, 'if an individual manifests religious views that are contrary to the values of the civic curriculum, then she or he may be excluded from teaching... because she or he is unable to affirm, in good faith, the values of the curriculum'.[7] Thus teachers may be expelled from their profession because of beliefs conscientiously held.

What is noticeable is that, when two apparent rights are pitted against each other in this way, there seems little appetite from the standpoint of law for any reasonable accommodation. The views of the state have to be applied regardless of any conscientious dissent. Yet the issue of freedom of conscience, and freedom of religion, arises in its most acute form when unpopular, or unfashionable, minority positions are in question. Freedom is safeguarded only when the majority allows beliefs to be manifested of which it disapproves.

Rights, in this instance those of homosexuals, often appear to trump any claim to a right of religious freedom. When such rights clash, it seems, the solution is for one to win, and not for any attempt to be made to satisfy both sides. It sometimes becomes very difficult to abstract the issue of religious freedom from the particular arguments of one impassioned debate. Yet the morality or otherwise of, in this instance, homosexuality is irrelevant to the dispute. Similar problems can arise when the argument is transposed to many other contexts, say in medical ethics. It is easy to imagine situations when the law allows a procedure (even euthanasia, or assisted suicide) that many doctors would want to avoid on conscientious, and perhaps specifically reli-gious, grounds. Yet it might be justified on the rounds of the equal right of everyone over their own lives. Is doctors' only choice then to obey the law or to give up practising medicine? Once again the issue is what happens when religious freedom is balanced against other apparent rights.

It is easy to champion the freedom of those who wish to act as we do. The problem comes when we fervently disagree with the stand being taken. It may still be important for the future of democracy, and the cherishing of human freedom, that we defend their right to disagree with us. Apart from anything else, we might one day find ourselves in a minority position, and find our rights challenged in a similar way. The question must be asked whether laws themselves should be drafted so as take account of conscientious objection. Further, should courts be more ready to find room for accommodation? If we really value religious freedom, including the right to deny all religion, we should be concerned if its claims are simply overridden.

Talk of exemptions, or accommodation, is never going to appeal to governments, unless they grasp the importance of the principles at stake. Simplicity in the law, and in its administration, will always be preferred, and a consistent application of a law will be assumed to be fairer. Yet, without exceptions, an unreasonable burden can be placed on religious believers unable to practise their faith. The example of the sensible law in the United Kingdom requiring motor cyclists to wear crash helmets is a stock example. It is a neutral law, not targeted at any group, and to be fair it should apply to everyone equally. Yet for Sikhs, with their requirement to wear a turban, it is unduly burdensome, and the law has granted an exception to them.

Much depends on how highly we rate individual freedom, and the freedom of institutions, particularly religious ones. When the issue of equality is to the fore, bringing in its trail appeals to human dignity, and human rights, it may be tempting always to override such considerations. Whether, and how far, that is justified is the subject of this book.

I

Does Religious Freedom Matter?

Is consent alone important?

It seems that, at least in the West, we are all liberals now. Liberalism is in the very air we breathe. The term can be ambiguous, although it is derived from the Latin *liberalis*, with its links to the idea of freedom or 'liberty'. We all tend to believe in the importance of the freedom of the individual. We respect the autonomy of others and find any form of coercion repugnant, particularly that of belief. We recognize that there have to be limits in the ability of the state to interfere with the lives of its citizens. As the political philosopher John Rawls held, liberalism sees all social cooperation as ideally taking place between persons who are both free and equal.[1] Such liberalism has deep roots going back to such philosophers as John Locke, one of the architects of the Glorious Revolution of 1688 in England, and an influence intellectually on the founding of the United States.

Some forms of liberalism, increasingly taken for granted in ordinary life, see individual autonomy, coupled with a respect for the rights of the individual, as the whole basis for any moral order. All obligations have to be consciously chosen. Institutions can be only validated through the consent of their members. Under this type of view, nothing is an obligation, unless freely and consciously chosen. Consent is all important. There is no given moral order into which we enter. One of the sources for the contemporary stress on the idea of moral autonomy is the eighteenth-century philosophy of Kant,[2] and his influence lives on strongly in both moral and political philosophy, not least in the work of Rawls.

The more the role of the individual is extolled, the more powerful the state has to become, since the role of any protective institutions, even that of the family, to act as buffers between the state and the individual is eroded. The picture is of equal individuals who can be motivated only by secular, and egalitarian, reasons, acting under the watchful eye of a supposedly benevolent state. Individual freedom is seen as the absolute precondition of democracy. It is what makes sense of any doctrine of human rights. As one philosopher, A. C. Grayling, points out, echoing a long line of such claims, 'if any idea of rights is to have content, the basic one must be liberty, for without it none of the others apply'.[3] Grayling himself, as a humanist, is contemptuous of any idea that 'nature or a deity has somehow magically endowed people with rights to life, liberty, property and happiness, when in fact the idea of these things is a human invention'. Indeed, he argues that their existence as right is simply 'the result of *decisions* to regard them as such'.[4]

A problem is that what we decide one year can clearly be changed another. Are basic human rights, whatever is to be included in them, simply the result of arbitrary convention? If so, those who dismiss them as Western constructions, inapplicable to countries such as China, would be proved right. Yet rights, for their potency, have surely to be seen as built into the very scheme of things. They are discovered, not constructed. At the very least, they have to be seen as being connected with our most basic nature as human beings.

Interestingly, Grayling himself rapidly moves away from the idea that rights are purely arbitrary conventions, such as which side of the road we derive on. He argues that 'experience and rational reflection show what is required to give individuals the best chance of making flourishing lives for themselves, and these framework requirements we institute as rights in order to make the chance of such flourishing available'.[5] Having therefore questioned the idea of natural rights, as instituted by nature or a deity (or 'nature's God'), he gets back in a few sentences to basic questions of what makes humans flourish. Since the answers may lie in the kind of beings we are, or in other words in human nature, it is apparent that we are quickly reverting to something approaching a view of natural law.[6] That would suggest that it is not totally under our own control what makes us flourish. Despite the stress on 'decisions', we are all subject to the constraints and opportunities given us by human nature. Rights depend on how things are, not on how we would like them to be.

Just as we cannot choose whether we need to eat or drink or find shelter, so there are many deeper needs that typically characterize our nature as humans. We can thwart those characteristics and fail to fulfil those needs or desires. Others may thwart them despite our wishes. Nevertheless, if we are each to fulfil our potential as a human being, we have to go with the grain of human nature rather than against it. This carries important implications for morality, but it also traces the importance of a concept such as that of freedom back to our basic nature. The very precondition of morality, and of rational thought— namely our freedom as individual human beings—has to be traced back to our basic human nature. We have the capacity to be free, and that capacity must be nourished if we are truly to function as the rationally responsible agents that all normal human beings should be. Slavery is wrong precisely because it ignores this.

Is religious freedom special?

The autonomy of individuals is clearly important, and many would question whether any special attention should be given to religious freedom, except as a species of a more general right to freedom of thought and conscience. Perhaps the importance of freedom of assembly should also be added to do justice to the undoubted fact that religion has a collective, as well as an individual, dimension. Freedom of belief implies also a right to freedom of worship, a much more public activity. The tendency, particularly marked in Europe, to widen the idea of religious freedom to that of 'freedom of religion or belief' suggests a reluctance to concentrate on religion, or the specifically religious conscience. The phrase 'religion or belief' is picked up in many contemporary pieces of legislation, for instance in the United Kingdom, but it leaves unanswered just what precisely is covered by it. It is generally agreed that it is difficult, if not impossible, to define religion in a way that does not already reflect particular prejudices. Reference to a belief in God, for instance, tilts the definition against polytheistic beliefs. As a result, courts across the world are always reluctant to get drawn into discussions about what constitutes a religion for fear that they will themselves get involved in overtly theological disputes. Yet adding 'belief' to the repertoire is not much better than hand waving. Not every belief can be protected in the way it is clear that human rights documents want religious beliefs to be.

One reason for adding 'belief' to the idea of freedom of religion is to make it clear that the protection of religion also applies to the protection of anti-religious views. Freedom of religion must protect those who reject all religion, as well as those who are committed to one. Humanists should be as free to argue publically against religion, as any evangelical to preach it. The problem is that 'belief' in these contexts will either continue to gain its salience from the meaning of 'religion', or be so stretched that it collapses into meaninglessness. Any strongly held belief might appear then to be a candidate for protection. That process seemed to be set in train when an English judge in 2009 held that environmental beliefs, about climate change, including beliefs about carbon emissions, should have the same status as religious beliefs. The case arose under the Employment Equality (Religion or Belief) Regulations of 2003 (themselves stemming from a directive of the European Union), and illustrates the vagueness of the phrase 'religion and belief'. The Regulations themselves explain it as 'any religion, religious belief or philosophical belief'.

Many wish to avoid this whole dispute by simply refusing to characterize 'religion' as something that needs to be given special protection. Why should religious (and quasi-religious) stances be given any more respect than any other conscientiously held beliefs? There are many who would wish to accord them less respect precisely because they regard religion as harmful, or irrational, or both. In societies that place so much emphasis on the value of individual autonomy and see that as the cornerstone of religious freedom, the stress is usually on individual belief. Much less attention is given to the corporate, or collective, aspects of much religion. It is very easy, given this background, to elide religious with other forms of personal belief, and to see religion as a particular case of the operation of the individual conscience when faced with basic questions about the ultimate meaning of things.

Once one treads this path, it can quickly appear impossible to defend religious freedom as such. One book on this theme is boldly called *The Impossibility of Religious Freedom*.[7] The writer, Winnifred Sullivan, drew on her experience of a Florida case concerning the kind of monuments to be permitted in a public cemetery. There were arguments about the religious symbols that families wanted to erect, and inevitably the case was drawn into reviewing how far a particular religion demanded certain symbols, and whether they were intrinsically 'religious'. Her own conclusion was that, simply because the court was drawn into individuals' idiosyncratic understandings, which were nonetheless important to them, it became impossible to make any meaningful distinction between the religious and the non-religious.

This may overstate the case, as there is a difference between an inability to make sharp distinctions and draw clear lines, and the lack of all distinctions. Different colour reds may shade into oranges, but that does not mean there is no colour red that we all can recognize. Sullivan points out: 'When law claims authority over religion, even for the purpose of ensuring its freedom, lines must be drawn.'[8] When law attempts to protect religion, it begins to enclose 'religion' with definitions that are often imposed from outside. Religion may be judged by external, and distorting, criteria. Realizing the danger, many jurisdictions lapse into vagueness, and are tempted by the references to 'religion and belief'. Yet that is to fall into the trap of assuming that, because distinctions can at times be difficult, the whole project of identifying religion becomes impossible.

Sullivan makes a more serious accusation about the effect of laws guaranteeing religious freedom. She points out that they mean that 'religion must prove itself as a social fact in court', and she sees the process as involving 'the subordination of religion to a secular legal authority'.[9] Her conclusion, given what she terms the 'anarchic folkways of US religion',[10] is that 'religion' can no longer be coherently defined for purpose of American law.[11] Given the prominence of the term 'religion' in the First Amendment, this is a conclusion with profound constitutional implications, and Sullivan pinpoints a major concern of many when she writes that the privileges given to religion are increasingly 'seen to violate the higher American principle of equality'.[12] Her argument continues: 'Unless "religion", is to be broadened to include everyone, to give legal protection to religion is to privilege those who understand themselves to be religiously motivated over those who understand themselves to be motivated by equally deeply held secular values.'[13]

This is an important challenge to anyone who feels that there is anything distinctively important about religious freedom. The assertion that the principle of 'equality' is 'higher' than that of religious freedom will also need justification. To decide which, out of religious freedom and equality, is more important, or indeed why either matters, demands considerable examination. In contemporary pluralist societies, where many religions, and many beliefs, have to coexist, it is not very persuasive simply to appeal to the obvious truth of a particular religion. Too many people in any given society will refuse to see it as true at all.

Does 'religion' matter?

Things are very different now from the eighteenth-century background against which the Constitution of the United States was drawn up in Philadelphia in 1787. Christianity, and Protestant Christianity at that, provided the backdrop, and was the major influence, whatever the differences of personal belief, and denominational differences. It cannot be taken for granted now in most Western countries that there is even a residual Christian belief, or even a general respect for Christianity, among all citizens. The advent of mass immigration by adherents of other religions in many countries has altered the situation further, and encouraged many to demand that religion should be regarded as a purely private matter and not a matter for any form of public recognition.

All this makes the question why, or whether, religion matters all the more crucial. 'Religion' is itself a blanket term, which covers myriad beliefs and practices. Not all of them will be acceptable in a civilized society, no matter how tolerant we wish to be. The extreme case of human sacrifice is an example. Nevertheless, just because some harmful practices arise from some religion, not all religion should be regarded as dangerous. Many identify religion as a source of division and strife in societies, and the history of the Western world can provide plenty of examples, as does the contemporary world. Yet the very fact that religion, in many forms, still presses itself on us in many parts of the world as a force to be reckoned with in the twenty-first century should give us pause for thought.

In the 1960s theories about inevitable 'secularization' were the rage in sociology. The idea was that, particularly because of the influence of scientific ways of thinking, religious belief would wither away, and secular norms would everywhere rule. The later Enlightenment's idea of rational progress would be brought to fruition. 'Superstition' would be vanquished. As people in the nineteenth century thought, human knowledge would bring 'improvement'. The natural sciences came to be seen as the best expression of autonomous human reason, and the idea of a supernatural authority came to be rejected by many.

Science, and secularism, were seen by many as liberating us from the restrictions of religion. For A. C. Grayling, secularism, freedom, human rights, and science still come as a package deal.[14] Yet religion appears resurgent in many parts of the world, and Western Europe, together with countries such as Canada, seem exceptions to a worldwide trend. It is not just Islam that is newly assertive in many countries. Christianity is on the increase in many parts of South America and Africa. Religion cannot be ignored. Its existence as an influence on human behaviour, for good and ill, is obvious in the present-day world. Decades of aggressive atheist government could not begin to eradicate it, as the experience of countries in Eastern Europe shows. After suffering persecution and coercion for over a generation, churches have been resurgent, and indeed, as in Poland, were often instrumental in the overthrow of Communism. Whatever the regime and official ideology, and however oppressive it may be, its role in human life cannot be removed permanently. Outward expression of religion may be prohibited, but the basic impulses remain, and eventually are manifested again.

Politicians have to take account of this. Any idea of freedom in the context of human society has to take a realistic view of what it is that drives all humans. Just as no policy can ignore the fact that people need food, drink, and shelter, it will be critically important to face up to the force of religion in human lives. If religious impulses are deeply embedded in our common human nature, the apparent universality of religion in all human societies will not be surprising. The Enlightenment prejudice in favour of science may still live on in some quarters, and anything that cannot be verified by science may be dismissed. In substance, this is the doctrine of logical positivism, long superseded in the philosophy of science. Science is made the arbiter of both meaning and truth, and everything else is dismissed as merely 'emotive', or completely meaningless (as A. J. Ayer, the Oxford philosopher of the mid-twentieth century, once used to do[15]). Old philosophical theories still echo in real life, as is shown by the remark that Thomas F. Farr makes. A former American diplomat, he has been particularly concerned with issues concerning religious freedom. He points out that a central aspect of the secularization theory that has been resilient among foreign-policy practitioners is 'the idea that religion is inherently irrational and emotive'.[16] It would follow from this view, he points out, that religious beliefs should have no greater influence on public policy than, say, alchemy. Once they are regarded as being merely personal, and private, aberrations, they can be ignored in understanding the policies of foreign countries.

The question is not, though, just about the pervasive influence of religion. It is about the consequence of its being a central component in human nature. Thwarting religious impulses could be as wrong as thwarting any other basic human need or interest. If they form part of what it is to be human, the simple act of blocking them for political or other reasons does harm at a fundamental level. The argument is that, given we are religious by nature, we have a natural right to follow our impulses. Following our nature contributes to our well-being and enables us, individually and collectively, to flourish. Not being able to express the deepest yearnings of our nature is harmful. The idea that we have, in this way, natural rights certainly influenced those who drew up the Constitution of the United States. Farr himself puts forward a similar view in defence of religious freedom, and says that 'to assert a right of religious freedom in this fashion is to affirm a claim about human nature and on behalf of human beings'.[17]

The idea is that religious freedom is a moral and political good, because the right to hold religious beliefs and put them into practice must be at the centre of what it is to be human. That does not mean that we cannot equally come to reject such beliefs. If we cannot live according to our judgements about what is most important in human life, and our part in some greater scheme of things, we are not really free to live our lives as we wish. Any doctrine of what it is for humans to be free has to take into account what it is to be human. Democracies have to accommodate disagreements even about this most basic of judgements.

The roots of religion in human nature

How can we say confidently that religion is part of human nature, if it is impossible to say clearly what religion is? Some think that the natural world is all there is, and others see the need to think of a realm of reality that somehow goes beyond, or transcends, our ordinary world of sights and sounds. Whether that encompasses all that can reasonably be called religious can be put on one side. An idea of God, or gods, existing apart from the natural world is crucial for much religion, and, when atheists call themselves 'naturalists' or 'materialists', it is this idea of the supernatural, or immaterial, that they are trying to resist. Coupled with it is the idea that we each as individuals matter so much that this life is not all that there is, but that there is some form of post-mortem existence. That in turn implies that, as humans, we are more than our bodies. Infused in such views is clearly the notion that there are deep underlying purposes in the world, perhaps emanating from outside the physical world, and that the world is not simply a blind process of cause and effect. Religion typically looks for meaning, and often claims to find it.

Can we move from vague generalizations about human nature, and learn from contemporary scientific research in this area? The so-called cognitive science of religion is a young discipline, drawing on insights in both psychology and anthropology. It is currently throwing light on the undoubted centrality of many of the impulses that help to form the foundation of religion. There can be arguments about why they are there, and how far they have been produced by the mechanisms of evolution. That is a different question from the contention it is a central part of human nature to possess certain cognitive tools that form the foundation of religious belief in every human society. They lead to common impulses that even atheists will share, even if they come to different higher level judgements from religious believers about their significance.

Alvin Plantinga, a leading contemporary philosopher of religion, claims that humans have a natural apprehension of the divine. He says that the basic idea is 'that there is a kind of faculty or cognitive mechanism, what Calvin calls a *sensus divinitatis*, a general sense of the numinous, which is a starting-point, and not the conclusion of reflective argument'.[18] The belief in the transcendent is thus as natural a part of our understanding as the perception of the trees outside my window, or my memory of what I had for breakfast. I can be mistaken about the reliability of the experience, but the experiences are basic, and not arrived at by reason, nor based on further evidence. In many ways, the cognitive science of religion provides backing for this kind of view, though a general sense of the numinous is less specific than an experience purporting to be of the presence of the Christian God. There is still plenty of room for the religious diversity that is an undoubted fact about humans. Cognitive science would also tend to suggest that the various cognitive tools that go to make up religious belief are not special to religion and typically develop as a part of a wider cognitive repertoire.

A basic substratum of understanding, which is built into us, makes it very easy to think of supernatural minds and supernatural agency. Stories and doctrines about gods and spirits are very easy to disseminate among human beings. Their minds are ready to seize on them. Cognitive science sees itself as providing evidence for the mental tools that humans characteristically possess. One such tool has received the acronym of HADD—the hypersensitive agent detection device. Justin Barrett, a leading researcher in the field, describes this as a 'crude and non-reflective system for detecting agency'.[19] As he says: 'If you bet that something is an agent and it isn't, not much is lost. But if you bet that something is not an agent, and it turns out to be one, you could be lunch.'[20] In everyday experience, we all know how easy it is to jump at the rustle of leaves in a dark wood, or a bump upstairs in an apparently empty house. It is natural to wonder who or what is there, and assume the noise has been produced by an agent. What has this got to do with experience of the non-natural and the transcendent? The theory would be that this tendency to look for agency can result in unseen agents being posited, where there are no obvious agents. Angels, spirits, ghosts, and demons are some of the alleged beings that humans find it remarkably easy to conceive of, and to transmit stories about.

Pascal Boyer points out that we have the cultural concepts we have because 'the way our brains are put together makes it very difficult not to build them'.[21] For instance, the cognitive science of religion points out that religious concepts typically are 'minimally counter-intuitive'. The idea is that they are a class of concepts that are particularly memorable, and for that reason easily transmitted from person to person. They are for the most part familiar, but grab our attention because they suddenly depart from normal intuitions in some respect. It is easier to remember fairy stories about a frog that talks than about just any old frog. A frog, though, that departed from our expectation too much would not be *minimally counter-intuitive*. If it drove a car, walked through walls, had flapping wings, and was bright purple, it would be hard for our minds to grasp. A slight deviation from the norm is memorable. Too much deviation becomes hard to track.

Another important element in the building blocks for religion comes from what is called 'theory of mind'. We all have developed an understanding of other people's perspectives. A child has to learn that the perspective of others has to be taken account. Children have to come to be able to predict and explain action in terms of other people's beliefs and desires. Young children of 3 or so find this difficult, but a year later will be able to do so. At the earlier age they find it obvious that, if they know something, so will their mother. If an apple is placed under a cup while the mother is present and then moved to under another cup when the mother has left the room, 3-year-olds will be sure that their mother will know where the apple has been moved to when she comes back. A year or so later, however, they will understand that she will not have seen the apple moved and will still think it is under the first cup. They will have come to understand that she is not infallible.

As Justin Barrett suggests, if children see God anthropomorphically, one would assume that 'children begin by assuming that God's beliefs are infallible just like their mother's, and shift to claiming that God's beliefs are fallible just like their mother's'.[22] Instead, what is characteristically found is a continuing, and firm, belief in God's infallibility. At the age of 4 or so, children realize their mother's perspective is limited, but go on assuming that God's knowledge is not limited in that way. They say such things as that 'God sees everything', or even simply that 'God is God'.[23] Obviously young children's beliefs are influenced by those of parents and teachers. The point is not how they acquire a belief or whether it is true, but what they find easy to believe. As Barrett, together with other researchers, holds: 'For children to "get God right" all they had to do is to keep answering like a three-year old.' As they say, 'God's beliefs are much like the pre-representational child's understanding of beliefs', because they match the world.[24] The idea of omniscience, or something like it, is not a sophisticated philosophical achievement, but the natural result of the thinking of young children.

Ideas of infallibility, leading to those of omniscience, are not so surprising, given the way children's minds naturally appear to work. The conclusion of Barrett and his collaborators is that, 'in some respects, God concepts (and some other nonhuman agent concepts) may be more conceptually primitive, in part accounting for why such God concepts are so widespread'.[25] They are easy to grasp, just because they are a natural part of our conceptual framework. This is not an obvious conclusion. Philosophers have thought concepts of gods are produced by analogy with human beings, and then concepts of omniscience seem hard to account for. If our notions of the divine are built on projections from the human condition, and gods are moulded in our image, talk of the divine seems forced and unnatural.

The idea of disembodied minds, divine or human, appears curious if our basic experience is that of bodies. Dualism, the view that minds and bodies, or mental events and physical ones, are distinct and separable, may be unfashionable in many philosophical and scientific circles, but it is strongly suggested that we all naturally think like dualists. It is easy, for instance, to continue imagining the mental states of the deceased. Emma Cohen, an anthropologist, looking at spirit possession in Brazil, considers that the idea of migrating minds is 'catchy and memorable' (in other words, minimally counter-intuitive).[26] She adds that it is 'supported by a fundamental cognitive tendency to view ourselves and others as immaterial minds, or souls, occupying bodies'.[27] None of us normally identifies ourselves completely with our bodies without the benefit of philosophical argument. Dualism appears common sense, just because that is how humans naturally think.

The psychologist Paul Bloom draws a connection between a belief in life after death and what he terms our 'intuitive dualism',[28] seeing belief in an afterlife as 'a natural consequence of our intuitive Cartesian perspective'.[29] Because we start off with the assumption that body and mind (or soul) can each persist without the other, it is easy to think of ourselves existing in a non-physical state. Further, whatever is to be said ultimately about 'near-death' experiences, where people are typically ready to describe conscious states apart from their body, one striking feature is the ease that everyone has in finding such experiences intelligible. The idea of someone floating near the ceiling of an operating theatre looking down on his or her body may evoke different responses, but incomprehension is not normally one of them, except in a sophisticated philosophical sense. The idea of a spiritual, non-physical world, coupled with an idea of post-mortem survival, gives an important foundation for religion. Without a vision of human existence stretching beyond this life, the core of religious views of human nature has been removed.

Current theories about the social benefits of religion, coupled with evolutionary reasons for its persistence, point out that a belief in supernatural agents who know what we do, and can punish us, can be a powerful influence inhibiting cheating and deceit.[30] Clearly belief in a God who knows everything could be particularly influential as a method of social control, a reinforcement for altruism, and an encouragement for us to keep our obligations. 'Pure' altruism, contributing to the good of others at a cost to oneself, poses an apparent problem for evolutionary theory,[31] but it is an indispensable component of a properly functioning society. People have to be willing to keep to their obligations even when it is not in their own immediate interest to do so. Religion is clearly a force that encourages this, and some see evolutionary influences at work that support the persistence of religion.

The 'naturalness' of religion

The cognitive science of religion attempts to trace the cognitive structures of the human mind, conscious and unconscious, which make it easy for us to understand and to notice some things, and more difficult to believe others. Teleology, the identification of purpose, seems deeply ingrained in human beings, and this may explain why science sometimes finds it difficult to make headway against 'creationist' accounts. Our 'natural' impulses may not be infallible guides to truth, but they are the ones we are most comfortable with.

The American psychologist Deborah Keleman has produced evidence for what she terms an 'early emerging "promiscuous" teleological tendency to explain all kinds of natural phenomena by reference to a purpose'.[32] She continues: 'From preschool, children attribute functions to entities like lions, mountains, and icebergs, viewing them as "made for something".'[33] She reports that, confronted with questions about why rocks are pointed, 'children prefer teleological explanations over physical-causal ones, endorsing that rocks are pointy "so that animals won't sit on them", not because "bits of stuff piled up over time"'.[34] This is not just something we grow out of, and she presents evidence that 'when tested using subtler measures, adults...reveal a tendency to broadly explain living and non-living natural phenomena by reference to a purpose'.[35] In other words, as she says, it seems that humans keep to teleological explanation 'as a default' as they grow up. It is easier for us all to think that things exist and events happen for a purpose than to believe everything is arbitrary and pointless. A readiness to see purpose, or to look for an explanation, even in apparently random, tragic events speaks of the same trait. It is a natural tendency that makes a search for explanations in terms of gods, or God, very intelligible.

Concepts such as that of an all-knowing God, of disembodied minds, and of supernatural agency arise naturally from the way our minds work. As Scott Atran asserts, 'for better or worse, religious belief in the supernatural seems here to stay'.[36] Barrett comments that 'belief in gods in human groups may be an inevitable consequence of the sorts of minds we are born with in the sort of world we are born into'.[37] He goes on more controversially to speculate that belief in one God may be 'selectively privileged'.[38] Whether a vague 'religious' belief in the supernatural agency is ingrained within us, or whether we are more receptive to the idea of a single all-knowing, all powerful Being, the fact remains that such tendencies to believe seem to be the very stuff of human nature.

Religion, or at least the impulses that help to produce the characteristic features of so-called religious belief, is a basic component of humanity. Denying religious truth in an atheist manner is as sophisticated as any theological reflection on the significance of our impulses. We may not be able to demarcate religion with precision, but we can recognize common features, and 'family resemblances'. 'Religion', not atheism, is the default option that we begin with, and this explains the near universality, and the persistence, of religion in one form or another. This is not an argument about the truth (or falsity) of any, let alone all, religion, but one about its central role in much human life and understanding. In any case, religious freedom does not mean tolerating beliefs that are generally recognized to be true. The test of such freedom is always to allow religious practices that one does not share and may believe profoundly mistaken. They will still be of central importance for those holding them.

The basic impulses that help to form religion are at work everywhere. There will always be pressures inclining humans towards religious views of the world, as the impulses are inherent in human nature. With reference to the cognitive science of religion, Johnson and Bering ask us to imagine a generation that grows up without any religious reading or teaching. They predict that even so 'they would believe in supernatural agents, that natural events would seem to have meaning and purpose ... and that they would successfully curb their ancient primeval selfishness for fear of greater forces observing and judging their actions'.[39] The building blocks of religion would be back in place, because they can never be removed. The writers could have added that their empirical studies indicate that the secularization hypothesis has to be false. Religion will always be resurgent in any society. Contemporary Western Europe is untypical of the general experience of humanity.

We can all reason about religion, and even question the reliability of some of our basic impulses as guides to truth. That will involve free, public, debate. Arbitrary attempts to stifle basic religious impulses by restricting people's religious freedom will come up against basic facts of human nature. It is like starving people, or refusing them shelter. They are stopped from functioning as they would wish as human beings. In this sense, religion must be regarded as a basic human good, even if some of its manifestations are not good. Some may wish the world was free of all religion. They must be free to argue their case, but should not impose this view on others, or achieve part of their purpose by pretending that religion is a wholly individual matter of no concern in the public sphere.

We cannot pretend that religious concerns are just like any other form of conscientious belief. That is not the message of empirical studies, and it goes against all historical and anthropological fact. As Johnson and Bering assert, many modern institutions with their founding norms 'are in fact deeply rooted in local traditions that are essentially religious'.[40] They point out that religious traditions continue to underlie fundamental aspects of law and political discourse. Indeed one might add that those who forget this will misunderstand the significance of many social practices. The basic facts of human nature will always be expressed in any properly functioning society.

2

Does Equality Trump Freedom?

A theological basis for equality?

There is good reason to give special protection to religious beliefs, since they appear to be driven by impulses that lie deep in human nature. We may often be barely conscious of them, but they form a characteristic, and important, part of what it is to be human. Most people, however virulent their atheism on a rational level, may admit that, at unreflective times, they may react to their surroundings in ways that could lead them to think of supernatural agency, or purpose. The reactions we most naturally have may not, we could think, be rationally justifiable, but they come most easily to us. Rational argument, and criticism, are in fact at a different cognitive level from our instant reactions.

Religious practices have lain at the heart of most human societies, and attempts to marginalize all religion and to pretend it is of little account, or a private idiosyncrasy, are doomed to failure. Arguments about religion must take place in any democratic society. All views should be publicly expressed in public debate without fear of coercion or being muzzled.[1] Indeed the more false, or dangerous, some religious beliefs or practices may be perceived as being, the more important it is that they can be challenged in a rational way in the public sphere.

The fact that all views should be able to get a hearing raises a problem that echoes through all discussions about religious freedom. It is one of the most basic features of democracy that it treats all its citizens equally. All should be equal in the sight of the law. Saying this sounds trite, but does it mean that everyone's beliefs must be treated equally? Does it mean that the state should not show favouritism to any particular views espoused by its citizens? This is an impossibility, since any state must know, and be willing to teach, why equality matters, and why personal freedom is important. A state may reflect the democratically expressed views of its members, but it must ensure that they have been taught a proper respect for the foundations of democracy, why we should respect each other, and why all humans have an inherent dignity.

The idea of dignity is to the fore in human rights documents. The Preamble of the United Nations Declaration of Human Rights begins by saying that 'the recognition of the inherent dignity and of the equal and inalienable rights of all members of the human family is the foundation of freedom, justice and peace in the world'. Already, therefore, the ideas of freedom and equality are linked to the idea of human rights and to each other. Yet talk of 'inherent dignity' and 'inalienable rights' suggests a basic moral order in the nature of things, which can easily, and most plausibly, stem from a belief in God. The words recall the famous words at the beginning of the American Declaration of Independence: 'We hold these truths to be self-evident, that all men are created equal; that they are endowed by their Creator with certain unalienable rights; that among these are life, liberty and the pursuit of happiness.'

The writings of John Locke were a prime influence on Thomas Jefferson, the author of the *Declaration*, and he included Locke, along with Bacon and Newton, in 'my trinity of the three greatest men the world had ever produced'.[2] He had Locke's portrait on his wall at his home, Monticello, in Virginia. Yet Locke, despite his position as an Enlightenment thinker and the first British empiricist philosopher, was also a Christian philosopher and a committed member of the Church of England. He was able, for instance, to write a book entitled *The Reasonableness of Christianity*. His beliefs about human equality were firmly based on his theological beliefs. As Jeremy Waldron has put it: 'Lockean equality is not fit to be taught as a secular doctrine; it is a conception of equality that makes no sense except in the light of a particular account of the relation between man and God.'[3]

There are explicit theological roots for the ideas of equality that have influenced the Western world, and the question is whether they can long survive when torn from those roots. Jefferson himself was no orthodox Christian, but he was heir to a Christian heritage and saw the need to base ideas of equality, freedom, and human rights in general on the idea that humans have been created by God. He explicitly asks, in a phrase now carved in the majestic memorial to him in Washington DC: 'Can the liberties of a nation be secure when we have removed a conviction that these liberties are the gift of God?'[4]

The idea of a moral universe still resonated with Jefferson and his contemporaries, and he, for one, did not believe that human rights are important just because we, or some people, happen to have agreed that they are. Any idea, in fact, that such rights depend only on the fact of the drawing-up of the United Nations Declaration fails to take seriously even the idea of 'inherent' dignity and inalienable 'rights' that it proclaims. A religious dimension remains in the background. Without the possibility of justification, ideas such as human dignity, or the 'sanctity of human life', hover without visible means of support. One philosopher says that 'these concepts are not in need of further justification'.[5] Indeed, he holds that 'implicit in much Human Rights discourse is the view that central principles express ideas which *logically* cannot be questioned'.[6] Yet the state of the contemporary world suggests that many do question them, and fail to take them seriously. They need firmer foundations, as does the idea of equality itself. Stifling the free exercise of religion in the name of equality, as many, we shall see, are inclined to do, can involve attacking the roots of a commitment to equality.

Second-class citizens?

Religion is always a target of totalitarian regimes, which wish to control it if they cannot destroy its influence, and it was a particular target of Communism. The reason is that it provides an alternative system of influence to that of the state, proposing an authority to which the state should be subservient. It threatens to restrict the power of the state, and its leaders are judged by a set of standards they themselves cannot control. This can become institutionalized in a clash between church and state, and then it can become a power struggle like any other. More dangerous for would-be dictators is the appeal to transcendent norms, and a supernatural authority beyond this life. Even if they themselves disregard all that, their citizens may be so swayed by such appeals that they will resist, even to death. The fate of Christian martyrs through the centuries draws attention to this. The collapse of Communism itself, particularly in countries such as Poland, owed much to Christian witness.

Yet, precisely because of this appeal to a transcendent authority that demands whole-hearted commitment, religion is seen by many as inherently divisive, and itself the cause of strife, both within a country and between countries. It is seen as characteristically resistant to compromise. The preservation of liberty then appears possible only if the state does not itself become entangled in particular worldviews, or the support of one religion rather than another. Those whose views are not championed will say that they are being treated as second-class citizens, if indeed they are accepted as citizens at all. There have been many countries where citizenship and membership of a church were seen as synonymous. In earlier generations, to be Swedish, one would be a member of the Lutheran Church of Sweden. To be Norwegian implied that one was a member of the Church of Norway. Paragraph 2 of Norway's new 1814 Constitution gave this wording, continuing the state of affairs that had obtained under Danish kings: 'The Evangelical–Lutheran religion shall remain the public religion of the state. Inhabitants belonging to it have the duty to raise their children in it. Jesuits and monastic orders are not to be tolerated. Jews are still to be excluded from access to the Realm.'[7] Only in 1845 was this monopoly partially lifted so that an Act on Religious Dissidents recognized the right of a limited number of Protestant denominations to exist in Norway alongside the state church.

The public recognition of one religion or one particular Christian denomination by a state, in preference to others, does not of itself imply the existence of a monopoly, or lack of freedom for others. It depends on what form the recognition takes, and how much toleration there is of those of different faiths. That does not inhibit many from seeing any form of public recognition that is not shared equally, as unjust, precisely because it appears to tilt the influence of the state against the rights of all citizens to make their own commitments. It does not take the dignity of each person seriously, because it favours the beliefs of some against others.

If forms of legal or other coercion are involved, this is a crucial position. Yet the whole point of a democracy is to provide a way in which those of many differing viewpoints can live together. In any democratic country a significant number of people will disapprove at any one time of the policies of their government. People should not feel second-class citizens because the beliefs they share with others about political priorities have not won the day. The question is whether the political complexion of a country is any different from its religious one. Could a country proclaim a religious allegiance we do not share, without making us feel less able to identify with the country?

Many feel that there is a big difference precisely because religion is a major element in what people see as constituting their identity, one that is often more important than nationality. If my religion is bound up with who I am, unequal treatment of religion will be seen as unequal treatment of people. Some appear to matter more than others. Martha Nussbaum, the American philosopher, encapsulates this kind of argument when she observes of the United States that it is a country 'that has long understood that liberty of conscience is worth nothing if it is not equal liberty'.[8] She continues: 'Liberty of conscience is not equal, however, if government announces a religious orthodoxy, saying that this, and not that, is the religious view that defines us as a nation. Even if such an orthodoxy is not coercively imposed, it is a statement that creates an in-group and an out-group.'[9]

Many still want America to be defined by a certain kind of religious view. Indeed, a nation that proclaims 'In God we trust' on its coins, and 'one nation under God' in the Pledge of Allegiance, is probably proclaiming more than the 'ceremonial deism' that is sometimes admitted.[10] Nussbaum gives voice to a powerful current of liberal opinion, which gives pride of place to the idea of equality between human beings. The conviction arises from this idea of equality that it is wrong to 'discriminate', so that 'non-discrimination' between people can appear to be the public good transcending all others. This works out the idea that equality forms the heart of democracy.

For Nussbaum, equality goes with the idea of not being dominated, so that she says: 'A major part of not being subordinated will be to have equal standing or status in public affairs. Thus this conception is highly sensitive to dignitary affronts in the symbolic realm.'[11]

Major battles are fought in the courts of many countries about the propriety of wearing religious symbols, such as a cross, or being dressed in particular ways. Many in a secular state such as Turkey consider it important that all alike wear non-religious dress, objecting stridently when the wives of the president and the prime minister wear Islamic headscarves. Yet not to be allowed to do so involves for many an assault on their own identity.

The attempt to treat all people alike can make religious people feel that they are marginalized in their own society, because they alone are not allowed to dress as they wish. The drive for equality can produce resentment at the creation of apparently unequal burdens. The attempt to create a public sphere where everyone is treated in the same way can result in resentment by practitioners of a particular religion that their commitments are being ignored and that they are being treated unfairly and unequally. A concern for equality can visibly diminish religious freedom.

Does equality lead to secularism?

The aim of non-discrimination influences the attempt to restrict public memorials identified with one religion. It can lead to a strongly secular public sphere. Such cases occur in many jurisdictions, but a typical one involved the alleged preference for the symbols of one religion over another and the resulting perceived inequality of treatment of different citizens. It arose in Trinidad, an independent Commonwealth country, where the so-called Trinity Cross had been established as the nation's highest award for distinguished service or gallantry. An appeal to the Privy Council in London from the Court of Appeal of Trinidad and Tobago produced the declaration that the creation of the so-called Trinity Cross of the Order of Trinity breached a right to equality, to equality of treatment, and to freedom of conscience and belief, as set out in Trinidad's Constitution.[12] As the judgment makes clear, the Trinity Cross 'was perceived by Hindus and Muslims living in Trinidad and Tobago as an overtly Christian symbol both in name and substance'.[13]

Paradoxically it was the 'Cross' that was seen to be the Christian symbol, although the name 'Trinity' could also have been seen as objectionable. The problem is that the name of the country would have to be changed if that was regarded as offensive. That merely illustrates how the single-minded pursuit of 'equality' and an urge to root out all forms of discrimination and preference to some sections of population can involve a major assault on the heritage, and even the identity, of a country.

There is potential for a judgment like this, if applied in the somewhat different constitutional setting of the United Kingdom to ride roughshod over much that many hold dear. The Union Jack is made up of saints' crosses, of undoubted Christian origin. Respected awards for gallantry would have to be renamed, including, above all, the

Victoria Cross, and even the Elizabeth Cross, established in 2009 for the relatives of soldiers killed in action.

The urge to prevent differences within the population creating deep chasms between groups of citizens can simply become a national policy of discrimination against the identity of a different group of people. It will particularly target those who wish to express their religious beliefs by dressing in a particular way, or who set store by the traditional public recognition of particular symbols. 'Equal treatment' can produce a different group of people feeling discriminated against.

The search for equality can be motivated by an attempt to redress perceived 'disadvantage', legitimating so-called positive discrimination. The concerns of minorities are then given more attention than those of majorities. All should be protected from oppressive coercion, but the idea that offence felt by a minority should always trump the wishes of the majority raises issues about the nature of democracy. All citizens must be able to contribute equally to the democratic process, but minorities should not appeal to their 'rights' simply to get their way at the expense of a majority. People often resort to the courts to achieve what they know they cannot achieve by democratic means. The rule of majority can approach tyranny, and that must be stopped. Yet, in a democracy, everyone cannot mould the whole fabric of a society to suit themselves. If they themselves are free to reject religion or to espouse a different one from the majority, the question still remains whether in the name of equality they are entitled to say that the state cannot formally champion what they object to.

When considerations of equality prevent people from expressing their religion in a public manner, religious freedom is subordinated to equality. Does that matter? Ronald Dworkin, the liberal legal philosopher, sees religious freedom as rooted in a more basic principle of liberty 'that generates a more generous conception of the spheres of value in which people must be left free to choose for themselves'.[14] Freedom of religion then becomes a species of a wider 'ethical' freedom. With issues concerning sexuality and procreation explicitly in mind (such as, no doubt, the perennial problem of abortion), he insists that protecting religious people and practices involves discrimination in their favour, once it constrains the ethical choices of those who do not share that religious viewpoint.

Dworkin draws a distinction between a 'tolerant religious society' and a 'tolerant secular society'.[15] The former might see religious freedom as a special right reflecting the importance of religion. The latter 'does not, as a community, attach any special value to religion as a phenomenon'.[16] Freedom of religion is then important only because it is a species of a wider form of liberty. Dworkin bases his preference for a secular society on a strong notion of personal responsibility, opposing laws that 'violate dignity by usurping an individual's responsibility for his own ethical values'.[17] For him, religion is a form of ethical value, and for him a 'principle of personal responsibility' for such values is the touchstone.[18] People must be free to make autonomous decisions 'about why their life has intrinsic importance and what kind of life would best realize that value for them'.[19] If I accept that 'everyone's life is of equal intrinsic value' then I must accept the fact of others' personal responsibility, just as I want to claim it for myself.[20]

A strong doctrine of equality, 'the idea that the lives of others are of equal importance to mine', here coexists with what appears to be an equally strong ethical subjectivism, according to which judgement about the good or bad of certain sorts of lives is a personal matter. Dworkin finds it easy to bracket religious faith with this kind of ethical outlook, because he later asserts that 'we must build ... our collective endorsements of truth round the distinction between faith and reason'.[21] In other words, faith is not, and cannot, be rational (or claim truth), a view vigorously challenged through the centuries,[22] and still carrying with it a considerable amount of controversial philosophical baggage.

The view that every human life is intrinsically valuable, coupled with the idea that everyone has a responsibility for realizing that value in his or her own life, form what Dworkin describes as 'the basis and conditions of human dignity', and he sees the first principle to be an invocation of the idea of equality and the second to be that of liberty. He thus attempts to weld equality and freedom together so that they cannot conflict and so that 'they are each an aspect of the other'.[23] Yet any appeal to human dignity in this manner will always raise the question as to what grounds it. The liberal espousal of equality and liberty, while making religion a secondary matter for personal choice, cannot look to any traditional religious grounding for such notions.

What is Dworkin's reply to the demand for a grounding for such principles? He believes that they are shared by 'almost all of us, in spite of our great and evident differences'.[24] We are all (or most of us) liberals, and that justifies our liberalism. The principles are sufficiently deep and general 'so that they can supply common ground for Americans'. An assertion about the human condition can be reduced to a socio-logical commentary on how one nationality happens at the moment to view itself. Liberalism becomes a transient phenomenon of a particular place and time. The justification of human dignity, together with the demands of equality and freedom, has to be more ambitious than that.

Equal liberty?

Combining liberty and equality, instead of setting them up in opposition, appeals to legal philosophers, such as Christopher Eisgruber and Lawrence Sager. Religious freedom is then a species of a more general freedom, with no special status given to religion. Religious adherents should not be treated in an unequal way compared with others. For this reason, 'Equal Liberty' will insist on 'equal status for people with diverse spiritual views',[25] but will not side with those who are said to contend 'that religion has distinctive virtues that entitle it to special constitutional status'.[26] This is of particular relevance to the United States, where the Constitution does appear to pick out religion as being worthy of special attention. The 'Establishment Clause' may appear to restrict religion, and in particular its official recognition by the Federal Government, but the 'Free Exercise Clause' appears to identify 'religion', so as to give religious beliefs and their expression a protection other beliefs may not have.

Eisgruber and Sager want to give an account of religious freedom 'that is above all shaped by concerns of equality'.[27] That means that issues of equality are given priority over religious concerns. They ask how government should behave towards persons, not religion. They accept that religion is an important component of identity and well-being for many, but the crucial factor will be equal regard for all. For them, 'a commitment to equality lies at the heart of religious freedom'.[28] It cannot be an alternative to it. Certainly religious freedom cannot be a selective freedom held by a few. All have it, or it means very little.

Concentrating on the equality of persons holding beliefs rather than on the content of those beliefs involves being neutral to all beliefs, including, presumably, to beliefs about the importance of equality and liberty. Yet Eisgruber and Sager are preoccupied with finding 'fair terms of cooperation for a religiously diverse people',[29] and it is unlikely that they will venture to give any possibly controversial justification for belief in equality and liberty. They want to maximize agreement, so, writing in an American context about American law, they are content to point out that 'equality and liberty are bedrock principles of American constitutional law'.[30] That is hardly a relevant argument for non-Americans.

Many, beyond the United States are reluctant to give any special place to religion. Contemporary European thought, as it emerges in the judgments of the European Court of Human Rights, is preoccupied with the problems of pluralist societies and the consequent need to treat all citizens equally, whatever their beliefs. European case law suggests that 'pluralism' is deemed inseparable from the idea of a democratic society, with the same phrases picked up in a succession of cases. In a case concerning the refusal to register the Salvation Army in Russia as a religious organization, the court refers to its 'settled case-law', and goes on to assert that 'freedom of thought, conscience and religion is one of the foundations of a "democratic society" within the meaning of the Convention'.[31] It continues by admitting that, 'in its religious dimension', such freedom is 'one of the most vital elements that go to make up the identity of believers', but adds that is also precious to 'atheists, agnostics, sceptics, and the unconcerned'.[32] Freedom of religion is seen by the court to be a result of democracy, and perhaps a precondition of it, but is viewed as merely a species of freedom of conscience. Pluralism of belief has to be cherished, no matter what the beliefs are. Any idea that religion, as such, is of special importance is absent.

Concentrating on 'belief' and its manifestations can imply that all religion is a totally individual affair. The European Court deals with this, and, harking back to pluralism, states that 'the autonomous existence of religious communities is indispensable for pluralism in a democratic society'.[33] This still fails to imply any priority for religion. Although reference is made to Article 9 (on freedom of conscience and religion), the court immediately appeals to Article 11 of the European Convention on Human Rights, which underpins a right to form an association. It sees any restriction on religious organizations as essentially an attack on that right, which can equally protect non-religious ones. The crucial factor in the court's eyes is a right 'to form a legal entity in order to act collectively in a field of mutual interest'.[34] The exercise of that right reveals 'the state of democracy in the country concerned'.[35] Democracy is the test, not the flourishing of religion.

Should equality 'trump' freedom?

Religion, it seems to some, can be protected only by appeal to secular norms, such as the importance of democracy and pluralism. The Council of Europe is even more explicit in this. In a Recommendation concerning religion, its Parliamentary Assembly (meeting in Strasbourg and made up of parliamentarians from the organization's forty-seven member states across Europe) upheld 'the fundamental right of freedom of religion', but made it clear by implication that this right is not that fundamental.[36] The implications of the Recommendation, derived from a submission by a Spanish socialist, are relentlessly secularist. It sweepingly says that 'the legislation of several Council of Europe member states still contains anachronisms dating from times when religion played a more important part in our societies'.[37] We are told that 'the Assembly reaffirms that one of Europe's shared values, transcending national differences, is the separation of church and state'.[38] It is claimed that 'this is a generally accepted principle that prevails in politics and institutions in democratic countries'.

The idea is that citizens are not being treated equally if some religious viewpoints are given special recognition. Nevertheless, as a statement of shared values, as opposed to the aspirations of some, it is just plain false, in a European context, to talk in this way about the separation of church and state. Many European countries give special recognition to particular churches, and the religious basis of many states is a fact expressed in law. The secular attitudes of France, or of Spanish socialism, are untypical. Vigorous attempts are, however, being made to impose forms of secularism on countries such as the Republic of Ireland, and Malta, with strong religious traditions.

The bite in the Recommendation from the Parliamentary Assembly comes when the issue of human rights is raised. The theme of this book is that rights to religious freedom and equality can often appear in conflict. In such situations, one may well have to proceed on a case-by-case basis. Rights have to be weighed against each other in the light of the particular facts. Ignoring, or sweeping aside, one of the rights may create undue burdens. Both rights should be accommodated as far as possible. Religious freedom is a basic right that cannot simply be discarded because it competes with other priorities.

This, however, is not the position of the Council of Europe, which reproduces the view of the later Enlightenment that human rights and religion must be at odds with each other. The Council asserts: 'States must require religious leaders to take an unambiguous stand in favour of the precedence of human rights, as set forth in the European Convention of Human Rights, over any religious principle.'[39] Moreover the Assembly wants states 'to require human rights training for all religious leaders'.[40] Since religious freedom is written into the European Convention, it is hard to see how the menace embodied in the word 'require' in both instances can square with such freedom. The phrase even suggests a wish to control belief, as well as its manifestations. The state is encouraged to place constraints on what religious leaders can teach, and to give them 'training' in what their priorities must be. Such subordination of religion—any religion—to the interests of the state, even if apparently benign, must be the antithesis of real freedom. The idea that bishops and others should be made to conform to the views and wishes of politicians strikes deep at the heart of freedoms hard won over many centuries in Europe, in some places more recently than others.

The Council may have in mind oppressive and coercive features of minority religions, but it may also be that a secular agenda is here being pursued with determination, so that any religious objections to homosexual practices, abortion, and many other controversial moral matters are swept aside. This interpretation is given impetus by the final recommendation that member states gradually 'remove from legislation, if such is the will of the people, elements likely to be discriminatory from the angle of democratic religious pluralism'.[41] Religious principles must be abandoned in favour of the removal of some forms of discrimination, but not, it appears, of discrimination against religion. In the pursuit of equality, it seems, some beliefs are still more equal than others.

The idea that human rights are intrinsically opposed to religious principles founders on the fact that the right to religious freedom is itself enshrined as a basic human right. Considerations of equality are not the only reasons for limiting religious freedom, but, when they do clash with the right to that freedom, why should they automatically prevail? The right to religious freedom is designed to protect religious belief and its manifestations from any prevailing orthodoxy that may oppose it. Religious freedom is worthless if it is allowed only when it fits in with the prevailing assumptions, and current policy, of government. Religious institutions become particularly vulnerable. Paradoxically, this is explicitly recognized in the 1998 Human Rights Act in the United Kingdom, which was designed to bring into British law the rights laid out in the European Convention on Human Rights. Section 13 of the Act says: 'If a court's determination of any question arising under this Act might affect the exercise by a religious organisation (itself or its members collectively) of the Convention right to freedom of thought, conscience and religion, it must have particular regard to the importance of that right.'[42] Unfortunately, however, this accommodation is drawn very narrowly. It does not, for instance, protect a Catholic adoption agency that finds it has to close down if it is unwilling to offer children to homosexual couples against its principles.

The European Convention on Human Rights allows limitations that are 'necessary in a democratic society' or 'for the protection of the rights and freedoms of others'. The demands of equality can then allow the limitation of religious expression to a marked degree. Much discussion of human rights characteristically focuses on the rights of individuals, so that the rights of institutions may not only get in the way, but appear to act as a dangerous source of power over and against that of the state. Christians may find the modern democratic state unsympathetic to their institutions and their teaching, but other religions also encounter problems, not least Islam. Islamic family law, particularly involving the place of women, may run foul of contemporary 'democratic' notions of equality. Perhaps this is the kind of case that the drafters of the Council of Europe Recommendation were particularly concerned about. Similarly, the reluctance of some sections of Islam to countenance 'apostasy', the right of those born into it to leave, runs counter to all democratic ideals of citizenship. It denies the most basic ingredient of religious freedom—the right of an individual to choose to be committed or not to a particular set of religious beliefs. Any appeal to religious freedom will be complicated. Allowing a religious institution to organize itself as it wishes can involve a denial of the religious freedom of individuals that the state should protect. Yet interfering with the beliefs and practices of such institutions carries its own dangers.

Any state's attempt to control religion, in the name of ideals of equality, can challenge the very freedom on which democracy rests. Yet the problem is that the state may not always be wrong in doing so. The clash between freedom and equality is a real and important one, and cannot be resolved by a blind preference for either over the other. It is illegitimate to weight the argument in favour of equality, but it may also be dangerous to think that matters can be solved by ring-fencing all religion. There may be instances where any civilized state has to protect its citizens *from* some forms of religion. If, though, it truly respects the freedom of religion referred to in all human rights documents, it has to understand that it must call on very weighty reasons to do so.

3

Religious Beliefs and Institutions

Are religions chosen?

Human dignity implies that each person should be treated equally, so that everyone's intrinsic characteristics are respected. Racism is held up as a terrible example of what can happen when humans are not regarded as having equal worth but are treated differently on the grounds of characteristics that they cannot change. The pursuit of homosexual equality similarly often involves the assumption that sexual orientation is not under our control. Like race, it goes to determine the kind of individuals we are. Arguments will continue to rage about this, but, if this kind of criterion is applied to religion, it will appear that religious commitment is not fixed in this way, but we are, or should be, free to change it. It is not, therefore, as important for our identity.

Unless a strong form of determinism is true, holding that all our beliefs are subject to forces beyond our knowledge and control, religion must be a cardinal example of something we choose to be committed to. Even if we were born into a particular religious community, we, implicitly or explicitly, have to make a choice to continue as a believing member of it. The fact that some communities may not see things like that does not deny what most people see as an obvious and important truth. Whatever the corporate, communal, or institutional aspects of any religion, individuals have to commit themselves to it.

Particular religious beliefs are not indelibly written within us. We do not have to be Catholics, Muslims, Hindus, or whatever. We can change religion, or repudiate all such commitment. Parallels with race, or even sexual orientation and disability, do not then hold up. Our beliefs are the result of our free choice. The idea of religious freedom is built on this assumption. If we could not help having the religious commitment we do, or be able to change it, there would be little point in campaigning for religious freedom, or drafting laws to protect it. Religious freedom includes the freedom to choose which religion to hold to, and indeed whether to be religious at all.

This view that religion is voluntary has been explicitly articulated in the UK Supreme Court in a case concerning asylum for homosexuals threatened with persecution in their own country. Lord Hope drew the distinction between homosexuality and the holding of a religious or political belief. He referred to the fact that homosexuals are, as a group, 'defined by the immutable characteristic of its members' sexual orientation or sexuality'.[1] He comments that the characteristic is 'less visible than race, because it manifests itself in behaviour'.[2] He then goes on to assert that, 'unlike a person's religion or political opinion, it is incapable of being changed'.[3] The conclusion appears to be that it will, therefore, be more fundamental to a person's 'identity or human dignity'[4] than any religious belief, which can be given up.

This assimilation of religious belief to political opinion, however, may not do justice to some views of religion. It is at least arguable that many Catholics, Jews, and Muslims think that religious identity is not a matter of individual choice, but an identity one acquires at birth. This may mean that it cannot be repudiated. The idea that religion is the product of individual commitment, freely given, arose particularly from Protestant theology. It is now accepted by the Roman Catholic Church, which, at least from the time of the Second Vatican Council in the 1960s, has championed religious freedom, but many Muslim countries do not find it easy to come to terms with individuals giving up their Islamic faith.

We should, however, distinguish between the particular beliefs we have chosen to abide by, and the way, as we have seen, basic impulses constituting typical religion are built into human nature. Just because we may be able to withstand our impulses, they may still be deeply ingrained. A nurse may have to overcome a natural revulsion at the sight of blood. There may be good reasons for her wishing to do so, but that does not alter the fact of her initial disgust. We carry our nature as human beings with us, and the building blocks of religion are an intrinsic part of it. Particular religions may be chosen, but, it may seem, religious impulses, including a tendency to conceive of the supernatural, stay with us. Religion, as such, is a part of the human condition, whatever forms it happens to take, and it should be seen as much a part of a person's nature as race or any other inherited characteristic.

Do religious institutions matter?

Stopping the manifestation of any religion is itself a challenge to the dignity of human beings. It throttles an important part of their nature. There have to be strong reasons for doing so. Some, though, see each person as an autonomous subject, whose choices must be equally respected, whatever they are. For them human dignity is challenged when some choices are rated more highly than others. People are then not treated equally, or accorded their proper dignity. Equality of treatment becomes for many the essence of dignity.

This is central to liberal ideas about the importance of each individual person having an absolutely free choice about what is good. This can extend beyond laudable toleration of difference, to a more subjectivist position, according to which people should be free not just to pursue particular goals, but to decide in a strong sense what goals are valid for themselves. No one else can tell them that they are wrong. In that case, no religion can be given special recognition, with the state preferring one, perhaps for reasons of history and tradition. It also means that religious commitments, as such, cannot claim any privileged position. All commitments should be equally respected. If people claim that something is important to them, then, as long as they are sincere, it must be. When someone refuses to do something on grounds of conscience, that should be enough. Looking for religious reasons is redundant, and unfair to people who are not religious. The idea of religious freedom becomes just a species of the more general category of freedom of conscience.

In the case of religion, there is another problem. Liberalism protects the individual, and has little patience with the role of intermediate institutions, acting as a buffer between the state and the individual. Yet most religion has a strong communal base. Whether the Church, for example, is seen as the body of Christ, or simply a free association of individuals, it has, like all other religious institutions, to have an existence apart from that of its members. All continuing institutions make demands on their members and cannot just reflect their members' multiple idiosyncrasies. Without criteria of membership, and distinctive activities, they would soon cease to exist. They would have no distinctive character. The official beliefs of an institution may not coincide with those of all its adherents, but, particularly in the case of religion, it could not survive if it did not know what it stood for, and what it wanted taught to children. There have to be proper standards of belief and practice.

Even if a Protestant denomination may decry the need for creeds, it must still corporately stand for something and rule other things out. The less it does so, the less it is likely to last. The fewer beliefs it preaches, and the fewer practices it advocates, the less point it has for existing. Sociological research indicates that the stronger religious institutions are those that demand a high level of commitment and costly behaviour from their members.[5] The less that is expected, the less membership means, and the more likely a denomination is to shrink. It is perhaps for this reason that, in both Britain and the United States, mainstream Christian denominations have lost support. Evangelical bodies demanding that their members resist some contemporary mores have grown.

Whatever the truth of this, the character of religious institutions matters. They do not just reflect the beliefs of their members; they help to mould them. A right to religious freedom cannot only cover the right to freedom of conscience, but has to protect institutions. Believers will see them as repositories of truth, to be guarded and proclaimed. Without an institutional setting, no religious believer can hope to pass beliefs on to future generations, in ways that can last. This is true of all the achievements of what we term 'civilization'. Universities provide a secular example of institutions that help to preserve and transmit basic understandings.

Institutions, however, are often disregarded in the current philosophical and legal climate. We shall return in Chapter 7 to one landmark case (*Syndicat Northcrest* v. *Amselem*), which concerned the practices of some Orthodox Jews. It reached the Canadian Supreme Court, and in it Justice Iacobucci explained: 'This Court has long articulated an expansive definition of freedom of religion, which revolves round the notion of personal choice and individual freedom and autonomy.'[6] It followed from this, he claimed, that a court should be concerned with the sincerity of a person's beliefs, and not whether it chimed in with orthodox or usual thinking in his or her religion. If someone felt deeply about a practice, and it was connected with personal religious views, that was sufficient. This meant that the court was not required to decide whether a belief is so idiosyncratic that it cannot count as a religious belief worthy of protection. It did not have to rely on expert witnesses to tell it whether this or that belief or practice is required, or even customary, for Jews.

Should courts discuss theology?

Justice Iacobucci also said, in words that could be echoed in the United States Supreme Court: 'The State is no position to be, nor should it become, the arbiter of religious dogma.'[7] There is then no need for a court to enquire into the orthodoxy of any particular set of religious beliefs, judged by the standards of the religion in question. It brings the matter from a communal to an individual level. The court does not have to delve into theological issues it would not see itself as qualified to adjudicate on. It would be very dangerous for the institutions of any state, not least the courts, to start telling a religious community what were the correct beliefs and practices according to its faith, or, worse, that its whole faith was mistaken, or misguided. That could involve a secular ideology dictating to a religious one, with a government or courts re-educating believers to show them their 'errors'. It is surprisingly easy for a court to start articulating the assumptions of the day, and go on to dismiss religious beliefs, particularly if it is dealing with a perceived minority.

Lord Hope's judgment concerning asylum for homosexuals, already quoted, in the United Kingdom Supreme Court started off with just such a condemnation of whole swathes of religious belief that liberal opinion finds unpalatable. Faced with the fierce, and terrible, persecution of homosexuals in some African countries, he claimed that it had been 'fanned by *misguided* but vigorous religious doctrine' (emphasis added).[8] He explained that he was referring to an 'ultra-conservative interpretation of Islamic law', and 'the rampant homophobic teaching that right-wing evangelical Christian churches indulge in' in much of Africa.[9] It seems as if Lord Hope has crossed a line here between deploring the persecution produced under certain legal regimes, and condemning what he sees as the religious beliefs supposedly underpinning them. Recognition of the plight of homosexuals in some countries is one thing, but launching an attack on the content of particular religious doctrines would seem to be quite another. It goes far beyond the remit of any court, however lofty, to decide how misguided such doctrines might be. That clearly must be the subject of prolonged theological examination.

Once a government decides what believers should and should not believe, the stage is set, at the extreme, for the type of persecution many Christians and adherents of other religions have suffered at times in Communist China. A founder of the house church movement, Wang Mingdao, was arrested in 1955 and kept in prison for more than twenty years.[10] He was eventually forced to make a public 'confession', which started by his saying that 'as a result of the patient attitude shown by the Government and the education given me I have come to realize my errors'. His 'crime' was to refuse to modify his beliefs to suit the political stance of the government. He wanted to remain apart from the state-sponsored Chinese churches, whose beliefs, he felt, betrayed the Christian gospel as he understood it.

Religious freedom is at its most vulnerable when confronting the organs of the state. Not only has the state considerable power, but, if it has totalitarian inclinations, it will always resent the invoking of any other source of authority. Yet modern governments often recognize that they should pay lip service to the need for religious freedom. They know that is what their citizens want. In the case of Wang Mingdao's 'confession', he was pressured to say: 'Our national Constitution has a clear statement about religious liberty. The government has constantly pursued a policy of protecting the freedom of religious belief.'[11] The irony should not have been lost on his listeners. A man who had been arrested and imprisoned for his religious beliefs, and who was forced to denounce them publicly (although he was later again to retract his 'confession'), was compelled to say that people like him were free.

It is not surprising that courts in democratic countries are normally fearful of intervening in religious issues. One can see why a court concludes that, if something seems important to a person from a religious point of view, that must be accepted at face value, with the question of sincerity being the only one a court has to settle. It is not part of the court's job to decide how important to, and central in, the Jewish faith a particular practice is. It then does not matter if most Jews do not behave like that. All that matters is that some wish to. Yet the Canadian Supreme Court went further. We are told in the *Amselem* judgment that, 'because of the vacillating nature of religious belief, a court's inquiry into sincerity, if anything, should focus not on past practice or past belief but on a person's belief at the time of the alleged interference with his or her religious freedom'.[12]

The stress on the individual as the only authority on the character of the beliefs held could not be more pronounced. Not only is any reference to the norms of any wider community, or religious institution, ruled out, but consistency in one person over a period is not necessary either. My religion is what I say it is today, even if last year I said something different, and even if my fellow believers may disagree with me. Religion could not be defined more clearly as a private, personal, and subjective affair, shifting with time, and unconstrained by any need to be loyal to a wider community. Yet most religion is not like that. Religion is typically carried in communities, and individuals are members of wider religious institutions. Whatever Christianity is, it cannot be just what I happen to say it is one Wednesday just because I say it. Beliefs have a life in a social context, and, shorn of that, much of the social significance of religion must be removed. It is not just what I believe, but a question of which religious community, if any, I choose to identify with.

Religion and identity

A stress on the supremacy of individual judgement can be seen to follow from a doctrine of equal citizenship. The idea that each citizen has equal dignity and importance can slide into the view that all beliefs have to be given equal weight, simply because they are the beliefs of somebody. To decry those beliefs, or restrict their practice, could be seen as a slight on the individual. This becomes more plausible when it is accepted that religious beliefs are often important constituent factors in the perceived identity of someone. Although, as we have seen, this can be denied, the link between religion and identity can be stronger for some than the fact of their race or their national identity. It is a matter not of what cannot be changed, but of what I think most important in my life, and also the community with which I choose to identify.

Recognizing the important contribution made by religion to issues of identity, of how I see myself and what is important to me, and of the group of which I am a member, may seem to raise the profile of religion. One writer about the contemporary Canadian situation puts it this way when writing about how far legal exceptions should be made for religion: 'The requirement of accommodation may rest on the

view that there is something special or significant about religious
beliefs, that they are deeply rooted or an integral part of the individual's cultural identity or membership.'[13] This may appear to give grounds
for giving special attention to religious freedom, but it assimilates religion to wider concerns. Those of a secular disposition will immediately point out that many non-religious people have deeply rooted
commitments, and everyone has some cultural identity. The grounds
for paying attention to religion will also be grounds, because of the
demands of equality, for giving equal consideration to others. Again
the tendency will be to see things from the standpoint of the individual. Groups and cultures are important because they are important to
individuals. Minorities must be protected. Although this will include
the rights of religious minorities, it will be a protection of minorities
as such. The fact that they are religious will be seen as secondary. The
idea will be that religious practices are ultimately important because of
individual choice. They can have no intrinsic value from a public
perspective.

Canada, with its Charter of Rights and Freedoms, has been something of a pace-setter in these areas, but its example can show how,
even if parliament is still considered sovereign, it will become increasingly difficult for it to challenge the moral authority of apparently
dispassionate judges, supposedly unswayed by sectional interests. Even
if parliament still has the power to override a Supreme Court decision,
as Canada's does, it will be politically difficult to do so. This may be a
harbinger of things to come in the United Kingdom, with the establishment in October 2009 of its own Supreme Court apart from parliament, and in New Zealand, with its own new Supreme Court set up
in 2010.

The process can result in the protection of sections of the population, particularly minorities, from any undue burden produced by the
effects of an apparently neutral law, reflecting the norms of the dominant community. A good example of this was the case in Canada of a
Sikh boy who wore a *kirpan* to school, as is the Sikh custom. This is a
short knife, resembling a dagger, which must be made of metal. Not
surprisingly this ran foul of a school rule against knives and such weap-
ons. Occasionally the same issue has caused trouble in English schools,
particularly when there are concerns about the prevalence of knife
crimes by youths.[14] Should an exemption be given because of Sikh
beliefs? The Canadian Supreme Court ruled that 'a total prohibition

against wearing a *kirpan* to school undermines the value of the religious symbol and sends students the message that some religious practices do not merit the same protection as others'.[15]

The equality of beliefs, and of religions, looms large here, but, even so, in the end it appeared that it was not the Sikh religion as such that was being protected, but the individual beliefs of a boy. One Justice writes in judgment that, in order to demonstrate an infringement of freedom of religion, the boy 'need only show that his personal and subjective belief in the religious significance of the *kirpan* is sincere'.[16] It was the individual, and not the community, who was being protected.

In a liberal society, with a strong belief in the equality of all citizens, the protection of minorities may seem important. Problems come when protecting minority practices cuts across beliefs about how individuals should be treated. What happens when the beliefs of a community appear to deny the very commitment to equality which is being upheld? The position of women is particularly sensitive here. Aspects of Islamic *sharia* law seem problematic for precisely this reason, and, after an acrimonious debate in Ontario, it was made clear in 2005 that there could be no official recognition of *sharia* law to settle personal disputes over family matters.[17]

A stress on human rights always results in a focus on the direct relation between individual and state. The courts will tend to protect, within reason, whatever beliefs an individual has, without reference to the standards of any religious community. The ideal of equality is driving this, so that the beliefs of no one section of the community take precedence over those of another. For this reason, any sign of privilege for Christianity has been outlawed in Canada.[18] All individuals are to be left free to make their own commitments.

Courts are not going to enforce communal beliefs on an individual, and issues of 'orthodoxy' will be irrelevant. Indeed any court, particularly in Canada, is going to be reluctant to make any investigation into what beliefs any member of religious community 'should' have. As one writer puts it, Canada 'has a constitutional structure in which the individual's relation to the state is primary and direct'.[19] Any legal system built on the conception of individual human rights, enforcing the equal dignity of all, will come to operate in the same way. Communities, whether in the majority or a minority, will have to be seen as mere collections of individuals.

Several consequences flow from this. An obvious one is that 'the individual cannot be coerced by the state to fulfil faith-based commitments inimical to this relationship'.[20] Religious commitments have to take second place to the idea of equal, inherent human dignity that animates the Canadian Charter of Rights and Freedoms. It may be asked what this idea itself rests on, but it seems at times as if the Charter itself takes on the role of civic religion, and cannot be questioned. The identity conferred by being a Canadian demands allegiance to 'Charter values'. Another consequence is that, as no set of religious beliefs can be given any privileged position, any religious basis for public policy has to be repudiated. That would itself be to challenge the idea of equality, because it would treat some people's basic commitments as more important than others, and hence challenge the dignity of those in the minority.

The role of institutions

A generation ago, it was taken for granted that Canada was a Christian country, in a way that is not now possible. Indeed, as one writer mentions, 'just a century ago, the Minister of Justice of Canada reflected public opinion when he stipulated that Christianity was an embedded component of Canadian law'.[21] Now, however, only people are equal, with institutions and bodies of belief very secondary. The individualism of a rights-based approach inevitably erodes the power and authority of all institutions. Must this mean that religious freedom can be a property only of individuals, or is the nature of religion such that special recognition should be given to religious institutions?

Alfred Stepan has written about the connection between democracy and what he calls the 'twin tolerations'.[22] He sees toleration as requiring both freedom from religious interference for political institutions, and freedom from political interference for religious institutions. He defines the 'twin tolerations' as 'the minimal boundaries of freedom of action that must somehow be crafted for political institutions vis-à-vis religious authorities, and for religious individuals and groups vis-à-vis political institutions'.[23] The 'separation of church and state' depends on this kind of insight. It recognizes the dangers of too great entanglement of temporal and spiritual authority. Religion can be corrupted and used as the means for secular purposes, just as ordinary politics can become a vehicle for the exercise of power by what may be only a section of that society.

Yet, whatever the dangers, this, as Stepan recognizes, is not just an interplay between individuals. Whole institutions are involved. The very phrase 'separation of church and state' recognizes the existence of the church or churches, and not just individual Christians. Institutions such as churches need to exist. Otherwise one of the most important elements in society is undermined—namely, the nexus of interrelationships below the level of the state but forming a vibrant civil society above that of the isolated individual. The paradox is that, the more individual liberty and equality are proclaimed, the more government regulation proves necessary to enforce that equality. Freedom is diminished, as everyone is forced to behave according to state-enforced standards. In the name of freedom and equality, freedom is visibly curtailed.

The dangers are illustrated by a decision of the United States Supreme Court concerning the rights of organizations to set their own rules according to their own principles.[24] A College of Law, Hastings, within the University of California, will recognize student groups only if they abide by conditions that include the school's non-discrimination policy, tracking state law on issues concerning discrimination on grounds of religion or sexual orientation. The Christian Legal Society wanted to require members and officers to sign a 'Statement of Faith' and to conduct their lives in accord with prescribed principles, including a ban on sex outside marriage between a man and a woman. The United States Supreme Court, by a five-to-four vote, upheld the right of the college to prohibit any discrimination in membership by student groups, in the face of students' desire for 'equal access'. This rates equality considerations above any belief, let alone of a religious kind. The court treated the rule as being essentially neutral. It presumably means that a Republican student organization cannot bar Democrats from holding office and vice versa. This, however, hardly makes the rule more sensible. There is clearly a danger of people joining an organization, particularly a religious one, to undermine it from within. Secular values are being imposed on religious ones. Indeed, as Justice Alito points out in his dissent, quoting religious groups: 'It is fundamentally confused to apply a rule against religious discrimination to a religious association.'[25] Indeed, without the maintenance of some standards of belief, any religious organization will soon collapse.

Justice Alito saw all this as a restriction of freedom of expression, if it 'offends prevailing standards of political correctness.'[26]

Rights and religious obligations

If religion matters, so does the nurturing of religious institutions. Yet the thrust of a liberal stress on individual human rights to be guaranteed by the state is to ignore the role of such institutions. This may be part of a more general sweeping aside of civil institutions and of seeing the individual as having absolute priority, but it bears down particularly on religion. This is not to deny that there are problems when the norms of a particular religion clash with civic values. The rights of citizens may well be at odds with the obligations of a religion.

This was well illustrated in another Canadian case, with wider implications.[27] A Jewish husband had refused for fifteen years to provide a *get* (a Jewish divorce) in spite of having given an earlier commitment. His argument was that he was protected by a right to freedom of religion. As was pointed out in the judgment, he was not required by his religion to refuse a *get*. According to Jewish law, he was merely entitled to do so, but need not. Quite clearly, one of the factors that the Canadian Supreme Court found objectionable was that, 'under Canadian law, marriage and divorce are available equally to men and women'; as the court noted, 'a *get*, on the other hand, can only be given under Jewish law by a husband'.[28] This went against all notions of the sexual equality espoused by the state.

In cases of conflict between the perceived demands of a religion and the prevailing norms in society, should religions be 'ring-fenced' merely because they are religions? In this case, despite complications,[29] the court's finding on behalf of the wife was strongly influenced by a desire to uphold the equal rights of women in such circumstances. Human rights, as currently understood, were going to take precedence over respect for a religious conscience, even when what was at issue was a religious, not a civil, matter. The court was not prepared to allow religious practices that breached what were seen as the basic requirements of equality. As one commentator put it, the judgment arose largely 'because public policy supported the removal of barriers to religious divorce and remarriage'.[30] The requirements of public policy had to take precedence.

Certainly, in a dissenting judgment, Justice Deschamps saw things this way. He pointed out that there are no civil rules governing the absence of a *get*. The issue was a purely religious one. He says: 'the requirements for issuing a *get* and the consequences of not having a religious divorce are governed by the rules of the Jewish religion.'[31] He added that 'the state does not interfere in this area'.[32] Yet clearly the state was interfering, even though it was the religious not the civil rights of the wife that were in question. He pointed out that the state had adopted 'the subjective standard of sincere belief' precisely to avoid getting involved in issues of the priority of different religious rules, or, he significantly adds, 'between rules of secular law and religious rules'.[33]

The test of sincere belief could not on its own be a defence for ignoring civil law. Lawbreakers could then claim they were acting out of religious belief, even if it was one that no one else held and that they had not adopted until recently. Exceptions to an all-embracing law would have to be more tightly defined than that. Religion will either be dissolved into the shifting category of conscientious belief or be given clearer delineation. The meaning of a *get* cannot be understood outside the norms and practices of the community that gave rise to the rule. This might suggest that the general public and the courts of a state that is not Jewish cannot enter into a proper debate about the applicability and acceptability of a practice that is a matter for Jews. That is the beginning of a dangerous argument that would set all religious practices outside the scope of public understanding and rational debate.

Ring-fencing practices simply because they are religious, and then denying outsiders the right to criticize those practices, even when they apparently contradict the law of the land, could mean the breakdown of civil society into different factions, each with its own rules and without any common ground. Denying religion any privileged position, and making it conform to prevailing standards in secular law, seems equally unsatisfactory. The one position undermines the rule of law, while the second undermines the ability of religious believers to live according to their own principles.

The temptation will always be to assimilate the particular problems faced by religious organizations to those facing any voluntary private association. Freedom of worship can be subsumed under freedom of assembly. The right of religious believers to live according to their own beliefs can be assimilated to the right of any private club to make its own rules. The problem remains as to what happens when those rules conflict with current legal norms. The usual response would be that civil law has to take precedence. Interestingly, however, in a controversial case in 2000, the United States Supreme Court ruled that the Boy Scouts were constitutionally exempt from a New Jersey law prohibiting discrimination against homosexuals.[34] This was derived from the First Amendment rights of freedom of speech and assembly. These deal with institutions only by implication, but the Supreme Court, by this ruling at least, seemed to imply that 'expressive associations' should have as much freedom to order themselves as any religious institution, even though the free exercise of religion is given prominence in the First Amendment.

While a willingness to accommodate strongly held beliefs in any country may be welcomed, the blurring of any distinction between churches and similar religious organizations—bodies such as the Boy Scouts, and even ordinary clubs—in the end makes special provision for a religiously inspired conscience more difficult. The more bodies of different kinds there are that can claim accommodation, the less accommodation is likely. Exceptions to any general law cannot be granted on a wholesale basis without making a mockery of that law. There have to be special and pressing reasons for allowing that.

Could, then, religious organizations be sufficiently protected by liberties open to other groups? They could be seen as themselves mere 'expressive associations', and able to share in their liberties. This is closely allied to the view that religious freedom is dealt with by the notion of equal liberty. Religions, it seems, can claim freedom, not because they are religions, but because they have characteristics, which, by definition, can be shared by others. Religious freedom is then regarded, not as any special kind of freedom, let alone the root of all freedoms, but as an instance of a particular kind of democratic right. It would then be linked only to the features of a particular form of government, and a particular constitution, not to something fundamental in human nature. Its claim to universality would be fatally undermined.

4

Equal Beliefs?

Removing history?

Williamsburg, the colonial capital of Virginia, is still visibly one of the most historic parts of the United States. Here English settlers began to build a nation. It was here, indeed, that some of the most impassioned debates, not just about independence, but about religious freedom, took place. The Church of England was entrenched as the Established Church, and the College of William and Mary, still in a prominent position at one end of the historic area, was from the first affiliated to it. The present chapel, although much restored, dates from colonial times, and was even allegedly designed by Sir Christopher Wren. It is a building of great symbolism, bound up with the foundation of Virginia, and the travails that gave birth to the United States.

For this reason, a trivial incident in October 2006 became proxy for a much greater battle. The then president of the college, who has since resigned, removed the cross from the altar of the chapel, on the grounds that, in a public, state-funded, institution, there was no ground for setting a building aside for Christians. Any acknowledgement that the chapel was other than a building for the use of all would slight those students who did not see themselves as Christian.

This created a furore, as it appeared to repudiate the history of the college. Articles even appeared in the *William and Mary Law Review*, as major legal principles appeared at stake. There was the argument that any public institution appearing to endorse religion was violating the Establishment Clause in the US Constitution. One writer said: 'There is an enormous great difference between a public university having a chapel and having a Christian chapel.'[1] Yet this seems curious, since being inclusive to all religions still appears to shut out those of no religion. The very arguments that make a Christian chapel seem problematic apply with equal force to any religious space. If the argument is that religious people should be allowed free exercise of their religion, then why cannot this argument apply specifically to Christians? Having a Christian chapel does not preclude the provision of other places of worship.

More significant were the reasons the President of the College (Gene Nichol) had for moving the cross. As another writer, Gerard Bradley, put it: 'Nichol was motivated to move the cross by some idea about equality: everyone should feel equally welcome at the Wren Chapel. No one should be an outsider, or a "second-class" citizen.'[2]

This would stop all religious practices in public places, since by definition those who do not wish to take part in them are excluded. Yet not having them restricts religious freedom very significantly. Public ceremonies of a religious kind are barred. Christians are not allowed to display their faith communally in the institution in which they live. In this case, the public history of several centuries was ignored. The issue was not whether a cross should be displayed on an altar. The idea that this was an altar (or a communion table), or that it was a Christian building, was being repudiated.

As Bradley argues in this context, the ideal of equality can stifle public debate about an appropriate course of action. He says: 'When a certain conclusion or belief is communicated as a fact about *me*, or as *mine*, or as an opaque feature of my identity, considerations of equality and common courtesy rule out critical engagement of the proffered position. Challenging such a position is tantamount to disrespecting or even attacking the person holding it.'[3]

This is the nub of many issues concerning equality in religious matters. Religion is seen as so constitutive of identity that belief (or lack of it) cannot somehow be separated from the person. This acknowledges the importance of religion in people's lives. Yet the conclusion seems to be that religious views and stances can never be publicly challenged or discussed. This goes with the unargued belief that religious faith is not a rational matter, nor amenable to critical reasoning.

Public institutions, it seems, have in the United States to be purged of religion so as not to give offence. Yet, in so doing, grave offence can be given, and, in the William and Mary case, undoubtedly was. In the end, a compromise of a sort was reached, in that the cross is now on public display in the chapel in a display case, with a note explaining its history. It is a museum piece, rather than a religious symbol, and something profound has happened to the way the chapel is regarded. In the name of equality, it can no longer, it seems, be seen simply as a place of Christian worship, even if Christian services may happen to be held there at times, and the cross temporarily allowed out of its case.

The desire for equality drives out historical identity, and the particularity of institutions is eroded. Many want to become a member of an institution such as a university precisely because of its history, Yet the idea of equality makes institutions repudiate their history for fear of appearing exclusive. The more distinct an institution is, the more it may appear to shut out those who do not like its traditions. A dull uniformity appears to threaten a basic freedom of choice.

Diversity and multiculturalism

A question still remains. Is not the dignity of the individual person of supreme importance? Does that not mean that each person's fundamental beliefs (usually of a religious character) deserve equal respect? Even if we can decide which beliefs are fundamental for a person, equally respecting all such beliefs rapidly becomes incoherent, if that means regarding them all as equally acceptable. It is common, in the name of equality, to value and even encourage 'diversity'. This appears wonderfully open-minded and tolerant. We may even conclude that all religious beliefs are of equal value and importance, just because they are important to some individuals and those individuals are worthy of respect. In a muddled manner, this is what relativism has always preached, through its idea that what is valuable is so for those who believe it.[4] Clearly, though, the fact that a belief is cherished by someone says nothing about whether others should also see its importance. The view that religious beliefs must be treated equally can just as easily become the view that they are all equally valueless, and to be equally ignored in public. We cannot assess and value beliefs merely on the grounds that someone else holds them. Everything depends on their content. Many beliefs are contradictory, and, while it may make sense to say that we should respect the people holding them, it can make no sense at all to say the beliefs in themselves are of equal value, even when they cancel each other out.

What of the belief in equality itself, which some would allege is constitutive of democracy? It is a belief far from universally held, and

in need of considerable justification. Why are people to be regarded
as equal? Some may fervently believe in inequality. Certainly the
philosopher Nietzsche regarded any doctrine of human equality as
pernicious, since it holds back the strong for the benefit of the weak.[5]
We may, it seems, be faced with those who believe in inequality challenging those who believe in equality. Do we welcome that diversity,
and even say all such beliefs must be equally accepted? Do we say that
no belief must be given a privileged place, as that would demean those not
holding it? An attack on equality surely cannot be as valid as its defence.
If we were to hold this in the name of equality, it is difficult to see that
we really believe what we are saying. We are on the edge of nihilism,
according to which it does not matter what one believes. Even the
latter belief cannot be stated coherently without ruling out other possibilities, such as a belief that objective truth matters.

Beliefs about the equality of people cannot be developed into any
belief that all beliefs are equal. The status of individuals is very different
from that of the content of beliefs. The latter can be rationally assessed.
People as such cannot be. I can respect the fact that a belief is held and
matters to someone, without necessarily agreeing with the belief, or
having to accept it in any way. We can be tolerant of differences without
thinking that all diversity is to be welcomed. Some beliefs are foolish,
and disagreement for its own sake can be an obstacle to common action.
In a democracy, we need, as far as possible, to come to a common view
on what the public good consists in. The more respect for diversity is
preached as an end to be pursued, rather than as a means to rational
discussion and agreement, the less cohesive society can become.

So-called multiculturalism, according to which a diversity of cultures is encouraged in a single nation, has been practised in several
countries, such as Canada and the United Kingdom. Politicians now
recognize that in many cities it has produced distinct communities
which have little contact with each other and few common loyalties.
The idea of what it is to be British has seemed hard to define. Even the
need for a common language has not been pressed, with the result that
it is possible for some, particularly women, to live in an English city for
thirty years without learning any English. Some have tried to give a
rationale for this encouragement of diversity and respect for different
cultures, including religions. Yet, while the equality of all should be
defended, does it follow that all ways of life, and all differences of belief,
must be accepted, and even encouraged?

One writer who regards 'multiculturalism' favourably is Bhikhu Parekh, a political philosopher who is also a member of the British House of Lords. He regards moral and cultural diversity as an 'ineliminable fact of life'.[6] Parekh will not even allow an appeal to an underlying human nature, on the grounds, he says, that 'we have no access to it in its raw form and cannot easily separate what is natural from what is social'.[7] Modern developments in biology, and in the understanding of the human genome, might suggest that this underestimates the significance of simply being human.[8] Yet, despite this stress on the social, Parekh still feels able to talk about the value of being human.

Parekh produces three basic principles, which seem at odds with each other.[9] He believes that human beings have equal worth. He believes in the principle of human solidarity, and he also asserts the principle of respect for difference or plurality. He tells us that 'human beings have worth because they are capable of doing worthy things'.[10] Yet it is not clear, given his respect for plurality, how he can provide any universal standard of worth. He says that 'moral values have no foundations in the sense of an indisputable and objective basis, but they do have grounds in the form of well-grounded reasons'.[11] The problem is that, if morality cannot claim truth, or have universal application, reasons may not be rooted in anything other than historically and socially conditioned forms of life. We have the problem, particularly given his third principle of respect for difference, of how we can do anything other than simply 'respect' and accept beliefs of those who differ from us.

Parekh says that 'the ideas of individuality, choice, self-authorship, equality, autonomy and mastery of nature are historically specific and not inherent in human nature'.[12] This covers most of the concepts stressed in liberalism. It suggests, given the need to respect difference, that ideals of equality cannot be used to justify such respect, because of their historical specificity. Indeed he says that 'many religions do not value human equality and assign differential worth to different categories of human beings'.[13] Yet why should we not respect the views of those religions, in the light of the need to respect diversity? Parekh believes that principles such as 'equal worth' are important, but that does not stop him proclaiming that 'the diversity of perspectives . . . is a universal human good, which we have a collective interest in promoting'.[14] How he can be sure of what are universal human goods, when he has decried the idea of a universal human nature, and any

objective basis of moral value, is not clear. Parekh realizes that acceptance of diversity has its limits, because he says that 'this does not mean
that all forms of diversity should be valued'.[15]

We have then a multiculturalism that rejoices in diversity, but wants
to rule some things out. Yet diverse cultures cannot be accepted, if
they themselves challenge the basis of multiculturalism, even denying
the individual equality of individuals and the value of diversity. Parekh
denies objective standards, but looks for ways in which objectionable
practices can be criticized. He needs a standard such as equality to
underpin its acceptance of all cultures, but has to accept that not all
cultures value equality. There seems to be no way out of this conundrum beyond accepting that not all cultures and cultural practices
should be valued and accepted in their entirety. Some principles are
more adapted to human flourishing than others. Multiculturalism
wants to talk of the importance of equality, without being willing to
give priority to views that defend the notion of equality.

Norway and the European Court

The idea of valuing diversity in the name of equality challenges societies
where one particular faith has been dominant for centuries. Norway
provides a particular example. There the Church of Norway (*Den norske
kirke*) has played a central role in the formation of Norwegian identity,
and Norway has had a government-run Lutheran church since the Reformation, when Norway's Catholic bishops were ousted in 1537.

Major issues concerning the freedom of religious institutions are
raised by government control of the Church, however benign, and
theologians may well become uneasy about the subservience of the
mission of the church to the demands of the state. Contemporary
arguments in Norway, however, arise particularly with the idea that
people's dignity is eroded if their beliefs are not given equal weight to
those held by others. In Norway, this creates problems for a state that
has been explicitly Christian and has, in its schools, based its education
on Christianity. In 2007, 86 per cent of the population are said to be
members of the state church, and membership has long been very
much a badge of Norwegian identity.[16]

The Constitution, dating from 1814, states that 'the Evangelical
Lutheran Religion remains the official religion of the State'.[17] It further

insists that 'residents who subscribe to it are obliged to educate their children likewise'.[18] Indeed, until 1845, non-Lutheran Christians were regarded as criminals, and it was only in 1964 that all inhabitants were given the explicit right of free exercise of their religion. It has been easy in such circumstances to take it for granted that the country is a Christian one, with its Christian heritage reflected in the values permeating its educational system, and in the teaching of Christianity in schools.

In accordance with a 1968 Act, children of parents who were not members of the Church of Norway were entitled, upon the request of the parents, to be exempted from lessons on the Christian faith. Such children were offered alternative lessons in philosophy. This right of exemption removes the possibility of coercion or indoctrination, but that was not sufficient for the European Court of Human Rights. In a landmark judgment in 2007, the Grand Chamber of the Court ruled that this 'could not dispense the State from its obligation to safeguard pluralism in State schools which are open to everyone'.[19] Although pupils could be taught about Christianity, this had to be done 'in an objective, critical and pluralistic manner'.[20] Christianity should not be given any privileged position, let alone any assumption being conveyed that it might even be true.

A key phrase in the judgment concerns the so-called Christian object clause of a 1969 Act in Norway, echoed in a 1997 Act, which stated that 'the object of primary and lower secondary education shall be, in agreement and cooperation with the home, to help give pupils a Christian and moral upbringing'.[21] The Grand Chamber said that the relevant legal texts 'suggest that not only quantitative but even qualitative differences applied to the teaching of Christianity as compared to that of other religions and philosophies'.[22] While, given Norway's circumstances, there was reason for devoting more time to Christianity than to other religions, there could be no reason for suggesting that it was any way better than alternatives, or more important to Norway. The requirement of 'pluralism' in the court's view entails equal treatment of all beliefs. The state could not be itself committed to any.

This outlook may arise from a liberal view of the role of the state, but, in the case of Norway, it cuts across the history of the country and its own self-image. Substantial issues concerning national identity are at stake. The intrusion of an agenda based on human rights and the equality of beliefs challenges institutions in a way that cuts them off from their history. In this case, it is not a college that is affected, but a whole country. The judgment fed into major debate about the future role of the Church of Norway. Whatever its precise future relationship with the state, many in Norway still see it as a national or 'folk' church (a *folkekirke*), with a particular relationship to the Norwegian people.

This judgment was carried by the Grand Chamber, an assembly of all the judges of the European Court, by a majority of only nine votes to eight. Had one judge changed sides, the ruling would have gone the other way, and the ethos of a country might have been allowed to be significantly different. The minority issued a dissenting judgment contradicting all the basic findings of the court. They say firmly that, 'when devising the curriculum, one cannot overlook the many centuries of Norwegian history', and the 'long tradition' of Christianity in Norway.[23] They assert that 'conferring a particular public status on one denomination does not in itself prejudge the State's respect for parents' religious and philosophical convictions in the education of their children, nor does it affect their exercise of freedom of thought, conscience and religion'.[24] They deny completely that the legal framework 'implied qualitative differences regarding the teaching of Christianity as compared with that of other religions and philosophies'.[25] The particular subject in question ('Christian Religion and Philosophy') was an ordinary school subject, and taught as such, not in 'a preaching manner'.[26] The judges believe that the policy of partial exemption took full account of parents belonging to religions other than Christianity.[27]

Respecting people and respecting beliefs

Given such radical disagreement, even among judges, what are the underlying philosophical arguments for changing the nature of entrenched historical arrangements? Ideas of equality, and attacks on entrenched privilege, play a major part. The judgment of the court itself upholds the rights of minorities when it says that 'democracy does not simply mean that the views of a majority must always prevail: a balance must be achieved which ensures the fair and proper treatment of minorities and avoids any abuse of a dominant position'.[28] A main object of any emphasis on human rights is precisely to protect those who, even in a democracy, may be overlooked. The problem facing the court was how far a specific Christian tradition in a country could be reconciled with demands of modern doctrines of human rights, which rely on such concepts as dignity, equality, and the evils of discrimination. If every citizen deserves equal respect, and has an inviolable dignity, the argument will run, the views of some citizens should not be given a privileged position over those of others. All religious (and anti-religious) beliefs must have equal weight.

The problem is finding common ground in a 'pluralist society' where there is disagreement about education, or the public recognition of one religion or belief system over another. One Norwegian philosopher, Tore Lindholm, based in the Norwegian Centre for Human Rights in the University of Oslo, wants to draw on 'the modern tradition of internationally recognized human rights'.[29] He says that 'this tradition is rooted in an emerging worldwide public commitment to heed as inviolable the inherent dignity of every human being'.[30] Yet this is hardly a philosophical justification, but more a sociological commentary. If we look at the state of the world, it seems a forlorn hope, rather than a reflection of reality. Human rights need more than a shifting political basis. Lindholm argues that 'dignity is a value that may resonate within and across difference'.[31] By that he means that different religions, and other systems, may converge on a belief in it. That may sometimes be possible, but not everyone believes humans are so special as to deserve more respect than many animals. Some would say that was 'speciesism'.

Lindholm wants to ground the demands of religious freedom in 'human rights' and strongly resists the idea that the idea was fostered by Christianity. He maintains that from the beginning political protection of religious freedom 'was based not on religious principle but on the exhaustion of combatants absorbed in religious warfare between Catholic and Protestant rulers, during the sixteenth and early seventeenth centuries'.[32] He concludes that, 'disqualified by their performance in the European wars of religion, mainstream Christian churches had wasted their claim to a principal public role in the shaping of modern protection of religious freedom'.[33] Thus he believes a modern society has to be a secular one, where secularization is 'inseparably linked to the emergence of modern, universally applicable human rights to freedom of religion or belief'.[34]

None of this answers the question about the grounding of human rights, or why anyone should believe in inherent human dignity. Doctrines of toleration and freedom were, in any case, more rooted in

Christian soil than Lindholm admits. The experience of much of Europe, concerning the development of religious freedom, has been different from that of England and the United States, where the idea has had considerable intellectual traction, with religious inspiration, since the seventeenth century. Political realities may be a powerful driving force for people to accept ideas of religious freedom, but these ideas still need their roots in rational thought, and in conceptions of human nature.

A doctrine of human rights, stressing the equality of all, and the need to respect the equal dignity of all, may even cause problems for democracy when it explicitly champions the rights of minorities against the majority. The question is how far that challenge can go. In the case of Norwegian schools, parents should have rights of exemption from lessons of which they disapprove, because of alleged religious content. No coercion can be justified against a background of religious freedom. Yet should all beliefs be treated equally in the public sphere, regardless of how many hold them? Norwegian schools were being told by the European Court that they are not allowed to operate at all in accordance with the wishes of the majority. The humanist parents who initiated the court case were trying to change the policy of the state, against the wishes of the majority as to what should be taught.

The question of the future position of the Church of Norway has been the subject of anguished national debate, with issues of national identity in the background. A proposal for a new Article 2 of the Norwegian Constitution runs:'The value foundations shall remain our Christian and humanist heritage. This Constitution shall safeguard Democracy, Rule of Law and Human Rights.'[35] Even referring to a 'Christian and humanist heritage', itself a broad category, can seem 'shamelessly exclusive' according to Lindholm.[36] An argument based on equality would suggest that this does not embrace the equal dignity of citizens with different worldviews. Since this has been coupled with a proposed continuing position of privilege for the Church of Norway as the 'Folk Church', the argument has been that this refuses to put all religious beliefs on an equal footing, in the same way as the desire to give prominence to Christianity in the school curriculum. Lindholm sees many in Norway remaining in the grip of Lutheran state–church tradition, thinking that a prominent role for the Lutheran Church naturally arises out of Norway's history and Christian heritage.[37]

Two positions arise in the Norwegian debate that reflect a wider debate in Europe. On the Norwegian side, there is anxiety about the role of Christianity, as exemplified by the role of the state church, but not confined to that. On the other hand, ideas based on international standards of human rights proclaim principles based on dignity and equality, so that no one belief system can be given a privileged position over another. The argument may partly be about ceremonial declarations about the source of a state's values. It also, however, has very real consequences, above all in the content of the education given in state schools.

Should the constitution of a country be inclusive, accepting the diversity, pluralism, and multicultural reality of those who are its citizens? These words are all used when human rights are at issue. The idea is that any inclusive constitution must not identify with any one outlook. This appears to entail that all religions, and comparable beliefs, have to be equally respected. The ideas of equality and human rights go hand in hand, and the latter cannot be selectively distributed. We are all equally human. Even though respecting the people who hold beliefs is different from respecting the beliefs held, attacking a belief can sometimes seem an attack on the person. This is why, in any interaction between citizens, or between government and citizens, there are basic norms of courtesy to be observed. It is no accident that the word 'civility' is linked closely with the Latin word for citizen (*civis*). Living in a civil community (or a community of citizens) demands being civil (or polite) to one another. Hurtful and scornful attacks on beliefs, which may be very precious to those holding them, should not be a part of the democratic process. That is what respect for each other demands. It is too easy to give offence unnecessarily.

Yet, if no distinction is made between beliefs and the persons holding them, no belief can be rationally criticized without this appearing to be an attack on the person. That makes all rational debate impossible, and democratic politics would become impossible. Attacks on policies must be seen as distinct from personal attacks on the integrity and character of those putting them forward. Parliamentary procedure in the British House of Commons attempts to enforce such a distinction. The word 'liar' is regarded as 'unparliamentary', and Members of Parliament are not allowed to descend to such abuse in debate in the Chamber.

Is religion any different? Again the issue of identity crops up, together with the old allegation that religious beliefs are not susceptible to rational debate. The latter is the controversial philosophical position that religions cannot claim truth. The former suggests that religious beliefs constitute the nature of a person, and cannot be detached from that person's dignity. That entails that a person is so identified with a particular religion that it is impossible to change a religion, or even simply to repudiate it. To do so would be to become another person. It is no coincidence that some of those who are most vociferous in talking of the alleged offence given to believers even by rational criticism are opposed to the most basic element of freedom of religion, the freedom to give up, or change, one's religion. When I am partly defined by my religion, an attack on my religion is an attack on me. Apparently rational criticism can be construed in ways that mean that I am given grave offence.

The same kind of argument can also be used in the opposite direction. Much can be made of the notion of 'harassment' in law, so that religious believers who make their faith known can be seen to be 'harassing' others. The act of communicating beliefs that others may not share to them can be seen as an attack on their human rights, particularly if the beliefs go against the way of life of the people being addressed. Preaching in the open air can be seen as an intolerable intrusion on others' rights. If all beliefs are equally recognized, and must, in the eyes of the law, be treated equally, being told one's own beliefs and way of life may be wrong will be seen as a transgression of the demands of civility. The equality of holders of different beliefs transmutes into an attack on the possibility of public, reasoned argument in areas of fundamental belief.

Human rights protect people, not beliefs. Laws against blasphemy are seen by many to be inappropriate, since they ring-fence beliefs, instead of protecting people from the effects of religious hatred. A law against the incitement of religious hatred is preferred, and this reasoning lay behind the decision of the United Kingdom in 2007 to repeal its long-held blasphemy law, which protected Christian doctrine, and that of the Church of England in particular, from scurrilous attack. It had attempted to distinguish between rational debate and trenchant criticism, on the one hand, and attempts to denigrate religious beliefs in ways that are shocking, and often obscene, on the other. There was never any suggestion that the blasphemy law curtailed debate, and it was in any case rarely invoked. The main objection to a law that seemed intended only to maintain a veneer of civility in the discussion of religion was that it gave special protection to Christian beliefs.

What, then, about the protection of other religions? The solution, as so often when there is this kind of conundrum in a pluralist society, was to remove the privileges in question, rather than extend them. Equality was given to everyone, in that it appeared that all religions, including Christianity, were now to be equally vulnerable. Non-Christians did not gain, but they were to have the satisfaction of seeing that Christians were now given no more protection than they had. Needless to say, this was not what they wanted.

Equality of religious belief can be achieved in any society by ignoring all such beliefs equally, since they cannot all be equally accepted. Minority religions in Britain have long seen this danger. One writer on multiculturalism refers to the possibility of the withdrawal of state funding from so-called faith schools, the vast majority of which are Christian, either Anglican or Catholic. He writes: 'Most Muslims reject this form of equality in which the privileged lose something but the under-privileged gain nothing. More specifically, the issue between equalizing upward and equalizing downward is about the legitimacy of religion as a public institutional presence.'[38]

Respect for people cannot be translated indiscriminately into respect for all their beliefs. When all beliefs are equally respected, all will be equally ignored. A respect for diversity of belief must ultimately be meaningless. Beliefs cannot be equal, even if the people holding them are. In the case of religious belief, respect for all beliefs can result in contempt for them all. No one can deliberately entertain conflicting beliefs simultaneously. That is the path to insanity, because we would have to give up all claim to be rational.

5

Is Religious Toleration Enough?

Equal recognition?

Must beliefs of a religious or quasi-religious character be given equal treatment, simply because the people holding them demand equal respect? The issue is not just whether all are free to worship or not as they please, and otherwise to manifest their beliefs. Should some receive, either individually or collectively, any official recognition that is not given to all? The doctrine of human rights is tailored to safeguard those who may suffer from the 'tyranny of the majority'. Their rights have to be equally cherished. Even if they are in no way actually being coerced, the fact they are in a minority demands that they be accorded the same civil rights as the majority, but also that they are not made to feel less identified with the nation of which they are citizens. Those who are actively pursuing the ideals of equality, and, in the case of the United Kingdom, trying to implement legislation concerning equality, become especially concerned with those they regard as disadvantaged. Under the guise of positive discrimination, this can involve actively pursuing the interests of some at the expense of what are regarded as the privileged majority. This has led to a feeling by many British Christians that they are being actively discriminated against, compared, say, with Muslims.

The relation between a majority culture and minorities dissenting from it is difficult, even in countries where individual freedom is cherished. In England, after the terrible conflict of the Civil War in the seventeenth century, John Locke emerged as an advocate of 'toleration' of dissenters, and a strong supporter of the 'Glorious Revolution' and the accession in 1688 of William and Mary. Following the apparent efforts of James II to introduce an absolutist monarchy, strongly allied

to a restored Roman Catholicism, the subsequent Act of Toleration of
1689 marked a major step forward in the toleration of religious dissent.
'Dissenters', or 'nonconformists' (because they had refused to conform
to the Anglican Prayer Book, as laid down by the Act of Uniformity in
1662), became an increasing influence on English life.[1]

The Act of Toleration marked a major step forward in religious freedom. Indeed, it is claimed, 'the Glorious Revolution and the Toleration
Act of 1689 separated church from nation'.[2] This was an important step,
as it was finally recognized that one could be a loyal citizen without
being attached to the Church of England. National identity and allegiance to what was becoming just one Christian denomination, among
several, could not be confused. The continued restrictions on Roman
Catholics (although they were given wide toleration, despite legal limitations[3]) could be explained as stemming from a belief in freedom,
rather than the reverse. They were under suspicion because of their
association with what was seen as an attempt to establish an absolutist,
and Catholic, monarchy. Protestantism and a love of individual freedom
appeared to go hand in hand, and most of the pressure for greater religious freedom, and a respect for individual conscience, came from those
in England, and the American colonies, who demanded freedom to
worship as they wished. Baptists and Quakers were in the vanguard of
such agitation on both sides of the Atlantic.

The Church of England has always been, and remains, the Established Church in England, but this has rarely meant that it enjoyed any
monopoly in the country. There was continued Roman Catholic dis-
affection and agitation after the Reformation, and then the rise of
Puritanism brought pressures from another side. By the middle of the
seventeenth century, in addition to the Baptists and Quakers, new
movements such as Presbyterianism and Congregationalism were
solidifying. The Act of Toleration recognized that, from a religious
point of view, England was, and has remained, a pluralist society. In the
eighteenth century, new tensions arose after the Evangelical Revival,
and the growth of Methodism eventually produced yet another major
denomination. These divisions were exported to the American colonies, and their existence was an important factor in the formation of
the religious outlook of the new United States.

One advocate of liberalism, Paul Starr, ties the importance of guar-
antees of religious toleration and freedom of conscience with what he
terms 'the logic of liberalism as a foundation for a stable polity'.[4] The

fear of religious conflict and wars of religion can be a powerful motive for toleration. Starr continues by saying: 'Religious toleration serves not only to allow people to worship differently but also to reduce conflict, facilitate economic exchange, and create a wider pool of talent for productive work and the state itself.'[5] The point is that, as the nation becomes more inclusive, it can draw on a wider body of those who are regarded as full citizens, and ensure their mutual cooperation for the public good. The connection between religious freedom and economic freedom has often been remarked upon. Since genuine freedom is indivisible, it is very difficult for a state to allow freedom and creativity in one sphere while keeping control of another.

Starr also writes: 'By dividing religion from law—that is by excluding religion from any binding social consensus—states guaranteeing religious freedom allow people of different faiths to cooperate under a political order that does not threaten to extinguish any of the various theological doctrines they support.'[6] The crucial word in all this is 'binding', in that freedom inevitably demands freedom to dissent, or to opt out. Any form of coercion, as implied by the reference to possible 'extinction' of doctrines, is the death of freedom. What, however, is more problematic is the idea that religion has to be divided from law. Justice cannot show partiality, and so its administration cannot favour one faith over another. Neutrality in the application of law is not the same as neutrality in the basis of the law. Just because law has no favourites does not mean that it must exist in a moral and religious vacuum. Religion with, say, its passion for justice can still be a powerful inspiration. Allowing people to disagree with the assumptions of the state, to dissent, or to fail to conform, is not the same as saying that all beliefs are equal in the eyes of the state because the state itself stands for nothing.

Is real religious freedom impossible within a state that supports a particular religious outlook? At one end of a spectrum is a so-called theocracy, in which the authorities of a religion impose one outlook on a people. Laws become an instrument for enforcing the particular rules of one religion. Some Islamic states appear like that. Some Americans see any attempt to weaken the separation of church and state as a move towards such a position in the United States. Alan Dershowitz of Harvard Law School says in apocalyptic tones: 'Let there be no mistake about the ultimate goal of the Christian right: to turn the United States into a theocracy, ruled by Christian evangelicals.'[7] Presumably the idea is that, if American law is made to reflect Christian principles, non-Christians will be subject to unacceptable coercion. The other end of the spectrum is the ideal liberal state, apparently standing for nothing, but allowing the maximum freedom to its citizens to live according to their own beliefs. All religious beliefs will be equal in the eyes of the state. The problem is whether a state that achieves total neutrality about all fundamental matters must not stop caring about freedom. For a liberal, even toleration must have its limits.

Is religious toleration enough? The question echoes debates about religious freedom in the days leading up to the foundation of the United States. The English Act of Toleration was a major advance in the granting of religious liberty, but the very idea of it being 'granted', and of people being 'allowed' to worship freely and to dissent from the norm, implies that toleration is a legal concession, not a right. The fact that in England 'toleration' was still withheld from Roman Catholics illustrated the way in which the interests of the state were still paramount.

Toleration or freedom?

In England, subsequent progress to total religious freedom for all was measured and gradual. The situation was very different in the American colonies. The 1689 Act applied to them, but that became part of the wider debate over the following century as to the relationship of the parliament at Westminster and colonial legislatures. The Act was accepted by the General Assembly of Virginia in 1699, but a succession of proposed laws, establishing the Church of England in Maryland, were refused the Royal Assent because they failed to give enough toleration to non-Anglicans.[8] After the king had vetoed other bills sent to London by the Maryland legislature, a new Maryland Act of 1700 went so far as to declare that the Book of Common Prayer must be used in every place of worship, ruling out both Catholic mass and Protestant meeting. This was not acceptable to London.

Maryland is now celebrated as a cradle of religious freedom. Lord Baltimore had ensured freedom for all Christians in the seventeenth century. He wanted to attract English settlers of different backgrounds to Maryland, and, as a convert to Roman Catholicism, encouraged the immigration of Catholics. By 1689 the majority of the growing, but scattered, population was Protestant, but little pastoral care was available, with three Anglican ministers in the whole of Maryland.[9] It was a frontier society, with need for more systematic religious provision. To this end, the Church of England was formally established, with thirty parishes created and a tax, or tithe, instituted to support them. It gained some privileges, but not at the expense of the toleration of others.

Things had always been different in Virginia. That is significant, as its influential leaders, such as Thomas Jefferson, George Mason, James Madison, and George Washington, drew on their experiences in Virginia to determine the shape of the US Constitution. The Church of England had been part of the official fabric of society from the very beginning, with the founding of Jamestown in 1607 and the immediate building of a church there. Parishes were established through the colony, as it expanded, and several Anglican buildings from that era are still used for worship.

There was a positive side to this, as proper religious provision was guaranteed. Further, the parish 'vestries', composed largely of gentry such as George Washington himself, were not only given the responsibility for the provision of buildings and parsons, but were in charge of helping the poor and destitute, and for general parish welfare. Virginians proved remarkably willing to fund the parish system right up to 1776. We are told that 'Virginians taxed themselves more heavily for the support of the parish than for any other public purpose'.[10] The Church was a vital component of civil society, although, with growing numbers of Baptists and Presbyterians in Virginia, there was pressure for greater religious freedom, and resentment at being taxed to support the parish.

The prominent laymen controlling the vestries were doubtless content that there was no effective ecclesiastical control. Although the Church of England was an episcopal church, there was no resident bishop, and, theoretically, Virginia was under the authority of the Bishop of London, who was responsible for all ordination of clergy. The colony's governor had a greater role in practice than the bishop. Local vestries made the most of the vacuum in authority, and in effect took control of the choice and election of their ministers.[11] The result was a reduction of the freedom of the Church as an institution. It was in the hands of the same people who were responsible for the government of the colony.

Because of the way the Church of England was interwoven in Virginian society, those who were not committed to the Church of England were bound to feel marginalized, particularly as the full force of the English Act of Toleration took many years to be felt in Virginia. This

is illustrated by a present-day local history of the Fredericksburg area of
Virginia, which says: 'It is a little known fact that it was possible to be a
religious dissenter by an obscure Act of Parliament passed in 1689.'[12] The
account goes on to mention how a fine on one man for not attending
church was dismissed in Spotsylvania County in 1742 'on the grounds
that he was a religious dissenter under this act'.[13] The mere fact that
compulsory regular church attendance was being enforced at that date
may come as a surprise, and may go some way to explaining why the
demand for religious freedom was so strong some thirty years later. Yet
this account obviously sees the Act of Toleration through Virginian eyes,
both past and present, as an 'obscure' act of doubtful relevance to Virginia.
The fact that one of the most significant moments in English constitutional history made so little impact gives a further explanation for the
growing demand in Virginia for greater religious freedom.

Things came to a head in the convulsions over American independence. Ideas of 'dissent' and 'nonconformity' suggested that there was a
public norm from which some deviated. Was legal permission to follow one's own conscience, dressed up as 'toleration', sufficient recognition of individual freedom? Some citizens then appeared more equal
than others, particularly if there were religious tests for public office.

All this was crystallized in the debate over a Bill of Rights and the
new Constitution for Virginia in 1776. George Mason, from Northern
Virginia, drafted the Bill of Rights, which in turn influenced the even-
tual Constitution of the United States. At first he tried to codify the
principles behind the English Act of Toleration, while keeping the
Church of England as the established religion. The relevant article of
his original draft embraced 'the fullest toleration in the Exercise of
Religion according to the dictates of Conscience'.[14] Seeing that toleration was not enough, according to his vision of freedom, James
Madison revised the article so as to delete the reference to mere toleration, and put in a guarantee of the equal entitlement of all citizens to
the 'full and free exercise' of their faith.[15] As one historian said: 'By that
point, he could draw the distinction between liberty and toleration as
adeptly as anyone. The latter implied subordination of some groups to
others, the former implied an equality between them—at least that is
what people were beginning to say.'[16]

There was much debate in the Virginia Convention, meeting in
Williamsburg to draft a constitution for the new state. Eventually
Article 16 of the Virginia Bill of Rights upheld the equal entitlement

of all 'to the free exercise of religion according to the dictates of conscience'.[17] Toleration had given way to freedom, in the name of equality. The move to religious freedom in Virginia owed much to Thomas Jefferson, who was proud of his authorship of *The Virginia Statute for Religious Freedom* of 1786. Its sentiments reflect a trust in human reason, characteristic of Enlightenment thinking, but a reason grounded in God, and not antagonistic to religion. The first words of the statute proclaim that 'Almighty God hath created the mind free'.[18] It goes on to insist that 'our civil rights have no dependence on our religious opinions'.[19] That is not to deny that our rights may rest on religious foundations, but to insist that we do not need to subscribe to any particular faith to obtain our rights. There should be no connection between being a member of the Church of England and being able to participate fully in public life.

The individual conscience should be paramount, but Jefferson had a strong belief in the power of truth. Coercion was not necessary to bring people on the right path, since, the statute proclaims, 'truth is great and will prevail if left to herself'.[20] Free argument and debate will be a means of arriving at truth, and hence general agreement. Jefferson felt strongly that conscience, and inner belief, were inviolable and out of the reach of the state. Opposing, in his 'Notes on the State of Virginia', the idea of any religious test as a condition of obtaining civil rights, he asserts that 'the error seems not sufficiently eradicated, that the operations of the mind, as well as the acts of the body, are subject to the coercion of the laws'.[21] This anticipates the modern distinction, important in human rights law, of the absolute right to freedom of belief, compared with a more conditional right to a freedom to act in accordance with that belief. We shall return later to the issue of how viable that distinction is.

Equal freedom in Virginia

The effects of the debates in Virginia were widely felt, and still are. The fact that Jefferson and Madison were such towering figures in the foundation of the United States would ensure that their passion for religious liberty be reproduced in the US Constitution, and the Bill of Rights eventually agreed. One commentator reflects that the Virginia Statute 'serves as the model for almost every state-sponsored confirmation of religious liberty, its eloquent phrases echoing in constitutions around the world'.[22] Jefferson's idea that reason and free enquiry are the chief guard against error meant that he believed that a multiplicity of denominations was a good thing. He held that 'difference of religion is advantageous in religion'.[23] He agreed in this with Madison, who famously maintained in *The Federalist Papers* that the protection of civil rights and religious rights came from the same source. Society had to be broken up into a plurality of competing parts. As he puts it, security 'consists in the one case in the multiplicity of interests, and in the other in the multiplicity of sects'.[24] In other words, monopolies are equally bad, whether political, commercial, or religious. Competition is necessary even in religion. Jefferson and Madison held that the secure status of the Church of England in Virginia, with an assured source of funding, led to complacency, and indolence amongst the clergy.

In England, John Wesley's Methodism entered what was becoming a dangerous religious vacuum, as part of the Evangelical Revival. In America, a similar movement became known as 'The Great Awakening', and left an indelible influence on the development of the United States. As Jefferson puts it in his 'Notes on the State of Virginia', referring to the position after a century of Anglican monopoly, 'other opinions began then to creep in, and the great care of government to support their own church having begotten an equal degree of indolence in its clergy, two-thirds of the people had become dissenters at the commencement of the present revolution'.[25] As a desire for independence took root, the formal links of the Church with England, and the loyalist sympathies of many of its clergy, would not have helped. For many, particularly viewing the eighteenth-century Church through the stricter demands of a later and more evangelical outlook, complacency and indolence were indeed its marks. Yet there is another side to the story. It may have embraced a more rationalistic, and intellectual, approach to faith than was later popular. Even so, as one recent historian puts it, in recounting the ordinary work of parishes and parsons in that period: 'Virginia's Anglican establishment was alive and vital on the eve of the Revolution. Parish energy had not slackened. New parishes were being formed in response to population growth and mobility, and virtually all ninety-five parishes had resident clergy, the majority of whom were American bred.'[26]

While the structures of Virginian Establishment may have seemed unyielding, and more intolerant to dissenters than was the contemporary English norm, the gospel preached from Anglican pulpits was likely to be highly reasoned. It was influenced by the spirit of English latitudinarianism, which aimed to make the Church of England as open, and doctrinally comprehensive, as possible. John Locke was likely to be quoted. In this theological soil, a respect for reason was nourished that motivated Virginians such as Jefferson and Madison. Even Jefferson, for all his undoubted lack of Christian orthodoxy, retained a lively belief in the dependence of the world on the ordering of God.

Establishment can appear to restrict the very liberty that is asserted to be God-given, but removing the structures that support religious provision can contribute to the apparent irrelevance of religion in public matters. Liberty can appear self-sufficient, without the need of theological support. Many in Virginia later saw a social need for some support for religion to counteract what was seen as a breakdown of morality, particularly following the upheaval of the Revolution. The Virginian patriot Patrick Henry introduced a Bill in Virginia to replace the Anglican Establishment with state support for all Protestant denominations. This provoked Madison's *Memorial and Remonstrance against Religious Assessments.* One of his main arguments was based, not just on the requirements of freedom, but on the needs of equality. For Madison, the Bill 'degrades from the equal rank of citizens all those whose opinions in religion do not bend to those of the legislative authority'.[27] Giving the state power to recognize any denomination or religion, however inclusive the process, grants to the state a power it should not have. He invokes the 'late Revolution' to argue that it was important to make one's stand on principle against authority, once 'usurped power had strengthened itself'.[28] A government that could decide to recognize Christianity could equally decide to enforce a particular brand of Christianity. Once financial support for some establishment is demanded, the principle has been conceded that such support can be expected for whatever the government wills.

Madison brought the idea of equality centre stage by complaining that Henry's Bill violated 'that equality which ought to be the basis of every law'.[29] He continued:

If all men are by nature equally free and independent, all men are to be considered as entering into society on equal conditions; as relinquishing no more, and therefore retaining no less, one than another, of their natural rights. Above all are they to be considered as retaining an '*equal* title to the free exercise of religion according to the dictates of conscience'. (emphasis added)[30]

Madison is quoting from Article 16 of the Virginia Bill of Rights, passed on the eve of Independence. Freedom has to be spread equally. Some should not decide what is good for everyone. Each must be in an equal position to decide a personal religious commitment. The government cannot favour one denomination, or even Christianity as a whole, without setting itself up above the consciences of citizens. It may do so in a benign way, but, once such power has been given to government, it can be used in harmful ways. It implies, Madison believes, either that the 'civil magistrate' is a competent judge of religious truths, or that religion is being cynically used as 'an engine of public policy'.[31] Both are ever-present dangers even today. If religious institutions are used as instruments of benign government policy, perhaps to promote tolerance or respect for diversity, they are being subordinated to government in a way that creates an uneasy precedent.

Madison's strictures on the importance, for the sake of equality, of the independence of religion from government are often quoted in contemporary US jurisprudence, but are not altogether easy to apply with any consistency. He argues that we cannot assume a freedom to profess a religion we believe to be of divine origin, without giving an 'equal freedom' to those who disagree with us. Yet he immediately supports this by saying that the abuse of such freedom is an offence against God. 'To God', he says, 'not to man must an account of it be rendered'.[32] Assuming that this is more than a rhetorical device to convince his opponents, Madison himself is turning to a theological justification of freedom. The whole tenor of the fight for religious freedom and equality, indeed, was that all this stemmed from the inherent, natural rights granted humans by God. Without that background, appeals to freedom and equality made little sense.

Religious pluralism?

A constant theme in Virginian attacks on Establishment, surfacing in Jefferson and Madison, is that financial support by the state, coupled with inevitable state control, had led to the atrophy of the Church. Religious pluralism is seen as a good thing in itself, and, in fact, a necessary concomitant of a healthy state. No one should assume a monopoly of truth. All should start on equal footing with each other. The idea was that religious pluralism is itself desirable, as the inevitable outworking of the free exercise of individual consciences, and as a necessary stimulant to the flourishing of religion. This sentiment has often been echoed, particularly when people have been faced through human history with apparent corruption in a powerful church, or with the complacency of a religious monopoly that need not exert itself. However, religious divisions sit uneasily with any conception of one God who is the source of all truth, and many Christians were made well aware in the twentieth century of the hypocrisy of preaching a gospel of peace and reconciliation, when they are not at peace or reconciled with their fellow Christians. Christian disunity, it has often been pointed out, can itself appear to give the lie to the gospel that is being preached. Moves to Christian unity can themselves be based on principle. The dangers of the abuse of power, particularly in a situation of monopoly, are real, but so is the urge to witness to one, universal, and objective truth. The urge to defend freedom, and the urge to conserve truth, in this instance, as so often, can pull in opposite directions.

Whether we see competition between Christian denominations as a sign of health and strength, or as an admission of human weakness, we are still left with the question of the attitude of the state. Denominational rivalry may be one thing, but, with the increase in the presence of other religions, and the principled rejection of all religion, Madison's appeal to equality takes on a new meaning, which resonates far beyond the United States. He exposed the fact that 'tolerance' may seem magnanimous, but itself betrays an assumption that freedoms are granted, which should inhere in everyone equally.

A familiar theme in attacks on the establishment of churches in Northern Europe is that government support stifles the Church. The vigour of American religion in the twenty-first century is often compared favourably with the secularism, and accompanying indifference to religion, that is seen in avowedly Christian countries, as in Scandinavia. Establishment, as Madison held, can appear the death of real religion. Martha Nussbaum, the American philosopher, quotes Madison explicitly on this and says: 'If we compare the vigor of religion in today's United States, where every sect must compete for adherents, with the weakness and indolence of many of the established churches of Europe, which have lost public support over time, we can easily see the truth of his claim.'[33] We need, many hold, a marketplace where competition flourishes, and where consumers should be able to choose the religion that suits them best. This approach can easily be bound up with questions of equality. All sects must have a 'level playing field'. One should not be given privileges that others do not have. That would suggest the others are not equal in importance, or value. We are then told that this is in fact good for religion.

Assertions about the connection of Establishment to religious commitment are of dubious value. Many other historical and cultural factors, such as the effect of two world wars on Europe, come into play. Even in North America itself in the early twenty-first century, the experiences of Canada and the United States seem very different. Neither has an Established Church, and in both there is a similar range of religious choice. Yet religion flourishes more south of the border. It is just as complicated to compare the United States with the United Kingdom. The Church of England is established in England, and in Scotland the Presbyterian Church is recognized as the national Church of Scotland. Yet in Wales and in Northern Ireland there is no Establishment, the Anglican Church (the Church in Wales and the Church of Ireland) having long since lost its privileged position because of demands for equal treatment by other Christian denominations.

In Wales, particularly, there has in recent years been a steep decline generally in church attendance, and particularly in the influence of Welsh nonconformity, once a power in the land. This has not occurred in the absence of competition between denominations. Some may suspect, indeed, that it is partly because of it, because churches have not joined forces sufficiently to resist the rising tide of secularism in the country. In England, too, there has in recent years been an apparent decline in religious commitment, but it is hard to see that this is because of an absence of competition. Many of the Christian denominations that flourish in the United States have long been present in England. Most of them were exported to America from England. There must be other social and cultural factors at work.

Special recognition?

We are taken back to arguments of philosophical principle. Is it wrong for any religious institution to be singled out for special recognition? The spread of toleration in England from the late seventeenth century started with the presumption of the predominance of the Church of

England. As in Virginia, this ensured religious provision through the parish system across the nation. Should the contemporary Church of England be accorded any special privileges in a modern, pluralist society? Martha Nussbaum raises issues that many Americans find puzzling. She talks of the adoption of a 'public orthodoxy' in European countries, and continues: 'Even today, Europeans of the majority religion feel no problem when a crucifix hangs at the front of all public school classrooms in Italy, or when public money is used for support of the established Anglican Church.'[34]

The latter point rests on a major misconception of the role of the Church of England and its relationship with the state. The Church of England does not receive state funding, any more than the Episcopal Church in the United States does. Its buildings, many of them very historic, have to be maintained out of its own resources. Its clergy have to be paid out of the contributions of church members. Its historic endowments are no longer sufficient even to provide a pension fund for its clergy, as they used to. In all financial respects, it has to behave like any other Christian denomination.

Unlike the United States, Britain does support faith schools, and there are many state-funded Church of England schools. This is hardly surprising, as the church was running schools before the provision of universal state education, and the state made use of the existing facilities. Yet the state also funds many Roman Catholic schools in England, and is increasingly giving aid to schools founded by adherents of non-Christian religions. The issue of equality in an educational context is therefore raised, not so much about Anglican privilege, as about the propriety of the state favouring religion and giving it any special place in education.

The Church of England is not an arm of the state, as was made clear in a court case that reached the House of Lords. The dispute was over an obscure point of law under the Chancel Repairs Act 1932, and concerned the parish church in Aston Cantlow, in Shakespeare country near Stratford-upon-Avon. The ultimate issue was the public status of the Church of England. One Law Lord observed that 'the Church of England remains essentially a religious organisation'.[35] Even if it has public functions, such as responsibility for church schools or the conduct of marriage services, this should not be regarded as 'infecting the Church of England as a whole, or its emanations in general, with the character of a governmental organisation'.[36] The present-day distinction between parish council, as an arm of local government, and

parochial church council, dealing with church affairs, merely under-
lines this.

Lord Hope made a crucial point when he said: 'The relationship
which the state has with the Church of England is one of recognition,
not of the devolution to it of any of the powers or functions of
government.'[37] This brings us back to whether the state should recognize one set of beliefs rather than another. Is any such endorsement
justified? The United States continues to hesitate between a general-
ized recognition of 'one nation under God', of a theism of a fairly
unspecific kind, and the idea that equality demands official detach-
ment from religion.

The pursuit of equality, and its relationship with democracy, are
raised in an acute form by Nussbaum's example of crucifixes in Italian
schools. A case about this was initially heard by the European Court of
Human Rights in 2009, and, to the disquiet of many in Italy, the court
concluded that such display is incompatible with the duty of the state
to be neutral in the exercise of its public functions, particularly in the
sphere of education. Referring to *Folgero*, the case of Christian education in Norway, the court did not see how 'the display of a symbol
which it is reasonable to associate with Catholicism (the majority religion in Italy) could uphold the pluralism in education which is essential for the preservation of a democratic society'.[38]

The European Court in effect championed the pursuit of 'equal
liberty'. The public display of a crucifix met the same objection that
the very idea of toleration met—that it implied that the state stands for
a public orthodoxy. This judgment created tremendous disquiet
throughout Europe, since it appeared to challenge traditions and symbols held dear in many countries. Many national flags, including the
Union Jack, contain crosses. Ten European governments, particularly
from the Orthodox East, made representations to the Grand Chamber
of the Court, the final stage in the European legal process. That then
ruled by fifteen to two that the display of the crucifix was allowable, so
that 'whether or not to perpetuate a tradition falls in principle within
the margin of appreciation'.[39] The latter is the space allowed to states
to determine their own constitutional principles and laws—for example, in such matters as the separation of church and state. The court
recognized that there was no European consensus on such matters, and
distinguished between the display of a passive symbol, and any process
of indoctrination or deliberate proselytizing within schools. It pointed

out that Islamic headscarves could be worn in Italian schools, as well as other symbols of religious identity.[40] Much was made of the apparent assault on tradition, and a concurring judgment asserted fiercely that 'a European court should not be called upon to bankrupt centuries of European tradition'.[41] Judge Bonello said that 'this Court ought to be ever cautious in taking liberties with other people's liberties, including the liberty of cherishing their own cultural imprinting'.[42] More crucially, the issue was raised of what precisely is implied by the protection of 'freedom of religion', as mandated by the European Convention. The judge referred to values, such as secularism, pluralism, the separation of church and state, religious neutrality, and religious tolerance, saying that they 'are not values protected by the Convention, and it is fundamentally flawed to juggle these dissimilar concepts as if they were interchangeable with freedom of religion'.[43] That may be arguable, in that religious intolerance, at least, would seem incompatible with freedom of religion. Nevertheless the point is clear: that freedom implies lack of coercion, such as indoctrination. Suggesting that it implies the absence of religious symbols in public relies on other doctrines. The liberal ideal of the equality of all beliefs and of the absence of public orthodoxy can itself take on the status of an orthodoxy, which can be potentially oppressive.

Even more fundamental, however, is the ground on which the ideals of freedom and equality are to be defended, if religious support is repudiated. This was a major issue in the case about the crucifix. The Grand Chamber quotes the Italian Administrative Court, which saw as central to the Christian faith 'the principles of human dignity, tolerance and freedom, and, therefore in the last analysis, the foundations of the secular state'.[44] On this understanding, a secular state should recognize its dependence on Christianity, rather than be opposed to it. While that may indicate how slippery a term 'secular' can be, it highlights a problem that will not go away.

6

Freedom from the Law?

Is the world 'disenchanted'?

Is religious freedom a privilege granted by a tolerant state, or a pre-existing right that should underpin society? We have seen how this question was keenly debated in Virginia, and it raises the question as to where ultimate authority rests. In the United States, 'we the people' were seen as the source of sovereignty, ordaining the Constitution. In a constitutional monarchy, sovereignty might be seen to flow down from the monarch, as the symbol of the historical experience of the nation, not up from the people. That would not be the signal for arbitrary tyranny, but a sign that the Crown is the guardian of constitutional freedoms, many established through long tradition. The monarch's duty is to uphold the laws of the people.

Whether in a republic or a monarchy, the principles that animate a state must be more than the creation of the legal arrangements of the time, or of the people who put them in place and administer them. However much is vested in the 'people', everything will depend on their character and the principles that motivate them. What do they rest on? A state's authority has often been understood as depending on something beyond itself. The transcendental basis offered by a religious appeal to God offers both an opportunity and a challenge to any state. It allows any state to offer a reason for obedience, in so far as it can be seen to embody the will of God. That can begin a path to abuse, as can be seen in 'theocracies', which identify the actions of a state too closely with what are purveyed as the requirements of God. Yet the apparent fact of such a transcendental basis can often also be a challenge, in that it gives an external standard against which the actions of a government actions can and must be judged.

Charles Taylor, the Canadian philosopher and social theorist, refers to the modern 'disenchanted' world, in contrast to 'the world we have lost' in which the social was grounded in the sacred.[1] He talks of how our new context has 'put an end to the naive acknowledgment of the transcendent, or of goals or claims which go beyond human flourishing'.[2] Appealing to human rights rather than to God gives us a more secular vision, but both appeals hold features in common. 'Human rights' constitute claims made upon any society, and are not graciously granted by the society. A human right strikes deeper than a mere civil right, which is a privilege of citizenship, granted by a government. Like God, human rights make their claim because they provide a standard against which societies can be judged. Totalitarian regimes may dismiss them as being Western constructs, and perhaps even vehicles of Western imperialism. The reason is that they do not wish their authority to be circumscribed by anything beyond their control.

The transcendental features of human rights may not be accidental. There is a real question how far the category of humanity, and hence universal 'human' rights, can survive in a 'postmodernist' age that views the eighteenth-century Enlightenment with suspicion because of its adherence to universal principles of reason and truth. The idea of a right as pre-social, and written into the nature of things, is reminiscent of the idea of natural rights, which had a theistic basis in the work of philosophers such as Locke. Once the world is truly disenchanted, the idea that nature carries moral import written deep in it seems hard to accept. It becomes just brute stuff, with no intrinsic purpose. The idea of human rights is more dependent on a view that God has created the world and people in it with an intrinsic worth than many of its proponents wish to recognize.[3]

This idea that societies are placed in a pre-existing reality that has moral import is still influential. It has conditioned ideas about religious freedom. This was most obvious in the views of those who drafted the Constitution of the United States, and the Bill of Rights. In a famous passage in his *Memorial and Remonstrance* James Madison said: 'Before any man can be considered as a member of civil society, he must be considered as a subject of the Governor of the universe.'[4] He concludes from this that religious allegiance must always take priority. He says: 'We maintain, therefore, that in matters of religion no man's right is abridged by the institution of civil society, and that religion is wholly exempt from its cognizance.'[5]

This is a ringing endorsement of the priority of the religious over the political, but it remains unclear how it should be interpreted when laws clash with a religious conscience. Should law be primary, or should religion? If allegiance to the higher authority of God should always have its way, the state should always give way to the demands of conscience. Yet the passage is sometimes read as maintaining that the law should be 'religion-blind', and should not take notice of religion at all. People should not incur penalties because of the religious beliefs they hold, or because of what they reject. Civil rights cannot be conditional in any way on having beliefs that meet the approval of the authorities.

We saw in Chapter 5 how Madison opposed the proposal in Virginia in 1784 to widen the previous establishment of the Church of England so as to levy a tax on all taxpayers for the support of 'Teachers of the Christian Religion', with taxes going to the denomination of the taxpayer's choice. Revenue collected from those who did not designate a denomination would be used for 'seminaries of learning'.[6] This explicitly involved the public recognition of the Christian religion, in a Protestant, rather than specifically Anglican, Establishment, with an opt-out for non-Christians. Similar systems operate today in some European countries, such as Norway. For Madison, the test had to be equal liberty for all. Religion has to be 'exempt from the authority of the society at large',[7] and hence from the legislature. There was a popular wish in Virginia that there should be no privileges, or penalties, attached to particular religious commitments. Religious conscience itself should be protected, and that meant putting it beyond the bounds of state control or official recognition. A natural right to religious freedom was not in the gift of civil authorities.

Must the law always be 'religion-blind'?

Could, though, religious people be granted exemption or exceptions from generally applicable laws, if they went against a religious conscience? This may not have seemed so pressing in a country whose legislators were explicitly motivated by Christian principles, and whose laws applied to a broadly Christian society, where the main disagreements were between Christian denominations. People may not have lived up to such principles, but by and large they were the only ones on offer. It is different in the twenty-first century, when political debate is characterized by deep disagreement between people with very different worldviews. The issue of the possible protection of a religious conscience from the impact of generally applicable laws has become a major problem.

Madison's approach of 'equal liberty' may seem attractive, but the principle of 'non-cognizance' of religion means that it is impossible to accommodate laws to the sensibilities of a particular religion. For many that is a recommendation, but, as some laws in different countries recognize by allowing forms of conscientious objection in various contexts, it can also create a particular burden on believers that others do not feel. There is a real issue as to how fair that is. It also appears to ignore the importance of the individual conscience, particularly in a democracy. 'One law for all' may seem to treat everyone equally, but, in so doing, it can bear down more heavily on some than others, if it stops them following their conscience.

For the law to be 'religion-blind', it is contradictory to recognize a religion even with the purpose of making exceptions in its favour. An American academic lawyer, Philip Hamburger, asks: 'Is the First Amendment's right of free exercise of religion conditional upon government interests?'[8] Is it an absolute right, or has it be limited by social considerations? An untrammelled right to do what one wants in the name of any religious principle could clearly undermine society, particularly given the kind of religious pluralism with which modern societies are familiar. Traditional Christianity itself can sometimes produce consciences at odds with social norms, as in the case of pacifism. There is now much greater likelihood of new clashes, and the question of possible limits to freedom of religion becomes pressing.

In talking of the difficulties about the free exercise of religion, Hamburger points out that 'many modern lawyers and judges assume that the right includes a right of exemption'.[9] The Founders of the United States were concerned with the removal of penalties, but many now see a right to free exercise as implying a right to opt out of laws, or to claim official exemption in particular cases. Instead of the law taking no 'cognizance' of religion, it now seems more pressing that it should not create undue burdens on some because of their religious beliefs. Times and societies have changed, but the widening of the idea of free exercise may be of concern to so-called originalists who want to base their interpretation of the US Constitution on its alleged original meaning, as clarified by the intentions of the Founders. Madison's *Memorial and Remonstrance* is still quoted in judgments of the US Supreme Court. In fact, however, the Founders themselves had different views about the place of religion in society, and matters cannot be settled so easily. The differences in approach between Washington, Jefferson, and Madison are significant ones.[10]

The issue has echoed down the subsequent centuries, with Madison's stress on the demands of equality regularly coming to the fore. It may seem fairer to ignore the religious beliefs of any given citizen, so as to treat all equally. Does not the rule of law itself demand absolute impartiality and equality before the law? The US Supreme Court itself proclaims on its portico the slogan 'Equal Justice under Law'. The lure of the idea of equality is strong. Indeed many would think that equality and impartiality are so built into the idea of law that the idea of 'unequal justice' has to be a contradiction in terms. There should not be 'one law for the rich and another for the poor'. The question faces us why there should be one law for someone with a particular religious faith and another for others. Should the law favour, say, Christians because they are Christians, or Muslims because they are Muslims? These are not abstract questions, as contemporary debates in many countries about the role of *sharia* law testify. If religious people are prevented from expressing their faith, or can do so only at great cost to themselves, that cannot amount to proper freedom of religion. The paradox is that this must involve identifying religious beliefs as such, and 'ring-fencing' their expression, and that, in turn, makes the state take 'cognizance' of religion.

The problem will be that courts in different jurisdictions must not just determine which beliefs are sincere, but also which are genuine religious beliefs of sufficient importance to justify special legal protection. Courts can then be drawn into theological controversies beyond their competence. No one would turn to a panel of bishops for a final ruling on legal matters, and there seems as little reason to expect that Supreme Court judges in any country can decide vexed theological issues. Yet they come very near doing so, if they are not careful. In American terms, the law and religion can become 'entangled'.

The question of exemptions from the law on grounds of religious conscience was a live issue in the United States at the time of the drawing-up of the Constitution. In a democratic society, it will normally be minorities that seek exemptions. A majority can ensure that they are protected by laws passed in their name. Minorities, on the other hand, can be at odds with the society they are living in, and be unpopular for that reason. They can even be targets of laws drawn up to restrict their activities. That can be exposed as unfair victimization. More intractable are cases where generally applicable laws are drawn up for what is agreed by a majority to be the common good, and yet a minority cannot conscientiously abide by them. The latter's loyalty to religious principle can even call into question their patriotism.

Conscientious objection and exemptions

Quakers in Pennsylvania during the War of Independence against the British were regarded with grave suspicion by their fellow citizens as their pacifism forbade them to take up arms. 'Patriots' and 'loyalists' were arrayed against each other within the colonies in what often amounted to civil war, so the Quakers' reluctance to fight made them appear to side with the British. The debate in Philadelphia on the issue brought to the fore two very different conceptions of religious freedom. The one that we have seen championed by Madison envisaged equal freedom under the law for everyone without distinction. There were to be no penalties (and hence also no privileges) because of religious belief. Yet the abolition of legal restraints did not suit the Quakers in Pennsylvania, who regarded the equal obligation to take up arms as an example, not of freedom, but of coercion. They were also reluctant to help fund any war, because of their principled objection to violence. There was a conflict between the interests of their country and the claims of their religion. The alternative view demanded freedom from the general law in matters crucial for one's religion. The law should not oppress any who in conscience could not obey it. This attitude would not impress many in Pennsylvania, who were prepared to risk their own lives, but then saw Quakers not only unwilling to do so, but also unready to give money to help the war effort.

Hamburger distinguishes between freedom under the law and freedom from the law, and summarizes what happened: He says: 'The Pennsylvania Revolutionaries were tolerant enough to guarantee a constitutional exemption from military service, but they were sufficiently attached to liberty under law to demand an equivalent from those who were exempted, and to deny that there was a general constitutional liberty from no-discriminating laws.'[11]

A religious conscience was respected, so that pacifists would not be compelled to go to war, and perhaps kill. They could not, however, opt out of their duties as citizens, and had to make a proper financial contribution in lieu of service. The law still applied to them. Indeed, Pennsylvania significantly went on to limit the rights of conscience in matters of religion to 'the free exercise of religious worship'.[12] This exemplifies a common reaction to the right of religious freedom. The more absolute the right is made, the more restricted the right becomes. The more expansively religious freedom is drawn, the more qualifications are built in. As Hamburger points out, looking at subsequent developments in US law: 'When the right of free exercise of religion came to be defined broadly, it was rendered conditional on government interests.'[13]

Democracies may value freedom of conscience, but no government is going to allow individuals or groups to opt out of general laws just because they do not wish to obey the law. A simple approach will be to say that in a democracy all may contribute (at least in theory) to the debates about which laws should be enacted, and all must abide by the result. That is what democracy means. The majority wins. Yet the ideology of human rights cuts across that, identifying particular interests that should be specially safeguarded. Religion marks out one of those special areas, both as part of a broader freedom of conscience, and as perhaps something to be cherished in its own right. It must be one of the building blocks of freedom that people can act in accordance with their most basic concerns.

One aspect of Madison's view suggests that religion must take priority over all social concerns. The obligations of religion, he believed, precede those of society. Yet, treating all citizens equally, without regard to their religion, seems to produce the opposite conclusion. As members of society, all must equally be subject to the same law. The removal of penalties for some religious views does not then mean giving privileges instead. 'Noncognizance' of religion means precisely that, and this can produce the idea that the state must be neutral to religion. It does not restrict religion, and yet it also cannot champion, or give favours to, particular religious positions. On the same argument, a neutral state should not look for a religious foundation for its laws, since they should be generally applicable. When religious opinions are discounted in this way, collisions between laws and religious obligations become more likely.

What then is the correct response for a democratic society, which claims to value individual freedom? Laws passed by a democratic process, and presumably with substantial public backing, demand acceptance by every citizen. On the other hand, the claims of religion have been traditionally seen as of crucial importance for individuals, and they also provide a test of how minorities are treated. Minorities are very often defined by their religion, which can be a cherished sign of identity. The treatment of religion typically becomes a test case for how free a society really is. Democracies can become elective dictatorships, coercing everyone into conformity with whatever are the prevailing norms.

There are fights for freedom of religion whenever social norms are imposed on religious believers who conscientiously wish to reject them. In Revolutionary Pennsylvania, the state insisted its laws applied to Quakers, but was willing to accommodate them to the extent of their offering payment instead of military service. There can be a wide area available for possible compromise. Yet no government could risk giving up, or qualifying, its authority in the face of conscientious objection of whatever kind. To do so in fact would be fatal, since it could not function if it could not collect taxes from citizens who objected to some policy or other. When a nation gets involved in a controversial war, many may want to extend their protests to withdrawing financial support. Marching in the streets may not be enough. Yet a government would soon become impotent if it accepted their right to do so.

Any government has to exert its authority, but that does not mean that some accommodation cannot often be made to respect people's consciences. A government can be gracious while still able to administer the law in the interests of everyone. Over the years, people have come to realize that forcing those who have conscientious objections to war to fight displays an unacceptable use of coercion by the state. Any democracy depends for its health on the moral consciences of its citizens. When they go against the settled will of the state, the state cannot capitulate, but ignoring them altogether ignores the source of a flourishing democracy. Respecting consciences informed by religious belief should be a matter of principle. It is, however, also a matter of practical politics, since those convictions are likely to be strongly held. A failure to accommodate them can itself help to build up serious resentment and discord within a country.

One issue concerning accommodations made for religion is whether these should be built into the law from the beginning by the legislature.

Must it be left to individuals to appeal to the courts when they
that their religious freedom has been impaired? Human rights cl
ters expressly protect religious freedom, and the latter should be a
feasible option. For the sake, though, of clarity, and to give democratic
ownership to recognition of a right of exemption, legislatures would
be wise to anticipate difficulties religious believers may have. No one
should assume that they can opt out of the legal system in which they
live. It is far preferable that the system recognizes their difficulties and
tries to meet them from the start.

A clash of rights

In many cases, different legal systems seem signally unable, or unwilling, to recognize the problems arising from religious belief. The most
difficult instances are always those in which there is a perceived clash
of rights, where, say, the right to religious freedom seems to cut across
demands for equal treatment. The issue of gay marriage, and of civil
partnerships, provides a good example of this. The current stress on
equality has been applied to issues of sexual orientation, and some
question why there should be a public recognition, and even celebra-
tion, of heterosexual relationships through the institution of marriage,
but not for homosexual relationships. This appears to involve an unequal treatment of individuals who have been promised equality. It is
said that their dignity is not respected. Yet people of different religions
sincerely hold that homosexual practices are immoral. They are following their consciences, and, while there is much prejudice in the
area, many are carefully coming to what they consider to be a reasoned
judgement on the matter, just as those who disagree with them would
claim to be doing.

Laws against discrimination on grounds of sexual orientation typically make no allowance for grounds of conscience. The analogy is usually drawn between this and racial discrimination. We would not think
it right to allow anyone to opt out of a generally applicable law outlaw-
ing such discrimination on the grounds that they sincerely believed in
the inferiority of some races, let alone that it was backed by some religious view. Yet, although attitudes in society are changing rapidly, there
is still much moral debate about the morality of homosexual practices.
Race does not normally lead to any particular forms of behaviour.

Sexual orientation might. Many might claim that there is a distinction between orientation, assuming that is fixed, and particular practices. Desires do not always have to be acted upon. Whatever conclusion is drawn on a very complicated subject, some would maintain that the issue is not which side one agrees with, but whether there is a genuine moral discussion to be had. Neither side should assume the other is so wicked that they have to be constrained by the law. Again the test of a democratic, but pluralist, society is how far it can contain disagreement, without one side simply coercing the other. The danger in this case is that, instead of the cruel intolerance towards homosexuals, which used to be encoded in law, we now have a similar intolerance to those who find that their religious beliefs forbid them from giving public recognition, and approval, to homosexual behaviour.

The issue is not which side is right, but whether religious, and similar, beliefs at least deserve the same kind of protection given to other victims of discrimination. Is discrimination against people because of their religious beliefs of no account, or, even if it is, should it be 'trumped' by other prohibitions on discrimination? All of these issues have been brought into sharp relief by a case involving a civil registrar in the London Borough of Islington who refused on account of her Christian beliefs to conduct civil-partnership ceremonies between same-sex partners. This became a new requirement on her when the Civil Partnership Act came into force in December 2005.

The registrar's case won the day in an Employment Tribunal, which held that, in balancing rights, one should not automatically trump another, and an accommodation should be found. On appeal to the next level (an Employment Appeal Tribunal), this decision was reversed, and the Court of Appeal ruled on the matter in December 2009.[14] The issue is such a symbolic one with wide ramifications that similar cases are bound to recur, in other countries as well as England. They capture the contemporary clash between a right to equal treatment and not to be discriminated against, and a right to religious freedom.

How much weight is to be given to each of these respective rights? The issue about homosexuality is irrelevant, although controversies about it cloud the issue. The more general question is whether a right to religious freedom must always be 'trumped' by other considerations. The conclusion from the London case must be that the right to religious freedom is cancelled completely when faced with the demands of equality. Yet, as the judgment points out, the Employment Equality

(Sexual Orientation) Regulations 2003, which prohibit discrimination on grounds of sexual orientation, do so in terms very similar to prohibitions of discrimination on grounds of religion or belief. Both need to be treated equally seriously.[15]

At this point, the distinction between belief and action comes into play, as the contention was that the London Borough of Islington was not concerned with the registrar's beliefs but only with her refusal to officiate at civil-partnership ceremonies. If she had been willing, that was all that mattered. We are told that 'Islington wished to ensure that all their registrars were designated to conduct, and did conduct, civil partnerships, as they regarded this as consistent with their strong commitment to fighting discrimination'. Given this aim, the court concluded that their actions were proportionate to their aim. The court, in a judgment given by the Master of the Rolls, held that Islington's policy of 'Dignity for All' was of overarching significance to the borough. He continues: 'It also had fundamental human rights, equality and diversity implications, whereas the effect on Ms Ladele (the registrar) of implementing the policy did not impinge on her religious beliefs: she remained free to hold those beliefs, and free to worship as she wished.'[16]

He stresses the fact that she was in a public job, working for a public authority: 'she was being required to perform a purely secular task, which was being treated as a part of her job.'[17] We are told: 'Ms Ladele's objection was based on her view of marriage, which was not a core part of her religion; and Islington's requirement in no way prevented her from worshipping as she wished.'[18] In a later paragraph the European Court of Human Rights in Strasbourg is invoked, when it is pointed out that the main sphere of protection is that of 'personal convictions and beliefs' and actions closely linked with those, 'such as acts of worship or devotion'.[19]

In European law, freedom is never unqualified in the case of religion, once one goes beyond the sphere of private, personal belief. In this case, the registrar is regarded as having an absolute right to believe what she wants, and to worship in accordance with those beliefs. When any greater freedom is claimed, qualifications are immediately invoked to restrict it. There are restrictions on how far belief can be expressed in action. A vexed issue is that the court explicitly makes a judgment about what her 'core' beliefs are. This is not just matter of her psychology, as it brings into questions theological issues concerning the core beliefs of Christianity.

Is any court qualified to decide what the core beliefs of a religion are? This is a recurring issue, but, in this case, it seems presumptuous for the court to view a Christian view of marriage as not a core component of the religion. The three judges involved in the Appeal presumably reasoned that marriage involves questions concerning practice, not belief, and of morality, not religion. Religious belief becomes restricted to narrow points about God, and religious practice to not much more than public worship. This definition of belief would be contested by many on theological grounds in more than one religion. Scriptural tags such as 'by their fruits ye shall know them' and 'faith without works is dead' only serve to illustrate a much wider conception of what it is to be Christian believer. The idea that propositional belief defines a Christian betrays an impoverished understanding of faith. Many philosophers of religion have gone to the other extreme, and stressed the importance of membership of a way of life, in which practice defines belief.[20]

The centrality of the role of marriage in Christian belief can hardly be doubted. It is viewed by many as a 'sacrament', and the relation between husband and wife is compared by St Paul with that between Christ and the Church.[21] The issue is theological and not legal, and Ms Ladele's views about marriage, as between one man and one woman, are not idiosyncratic. They are rooted in a recognizable pattern of religious belief. Arguments about the recognition of homosexual partnerships are sufficiently central for many Christians to split churches. In Ms Ladele's case, the fact that she was prepared to lose her job because of her beliefs indicates that they were central to her outlook.

The Appeal Court did not recognize that, although rights to equal treatment are important, respect for religious freedom goes to the heart of human rights. More broadly, the right to follow one's conscience has to be at the root of any democracy. It is what makes democratic consent possible in the first place. The claims of religion can be ignored through the common expedient of defining it too narrowly as doctrinal belief. Freedom to practise one's religion simply becomes freedom of worship. It is then all too easy for 'equality' to trump 'religion'.

7

Belief and Practice

Rights and limitations

All civilized society depends on restraints given by law. No one can decide to do what he or she likes, with no consideration for its effects on others. What, though, if a sincere belief means that one cannot obey the law? To be effective, the law has to apply to everyone. We cannot withdraw from our obligations as citizens just because of our conscience. The Quakers of Revolutionary Pennsylvania were made to understand that. In a democracy, people have to learn to live with laws of which they disapprove if they have failed to convince enough of their fellow citizens of the rightness of their views. Yet the issue of conscience remains, as the example of conscientious objection to war shows.

Democracies must tolerate the claims of conscience, because deeply felt moral and religious convictions provide the basis on which responsible decisions should be made. Morality has to constrain democratic discussion, so as to provide a vision for the kind of society to be achieved. Claims of conscience are the wellspring of democracy itself. Otherwise, society is the mere stage for unedifying power struggles, in which one section of society is often pitted against another to the detriment of everyone.

Yet this does not solve the problem about what limits there have to be for respecting conscience, and when individual consciences should be accommodated, and when not. The European Convention of Human Rights stresses the division between belief and practice. It seems to be a general tendency in many jurisdictions that, the more absolute a right to belief is recognized, the more the right to practise it is qualified. In the Convention, this division is explicit and intentional in Article 9 (already quoted in the Introduction), with a distinction drawn between the 'right of freedom of thought, conscience and religion' and, in the second clause the 'freedom to manifest one's religion or beliefs'.

Other human rights documents include the same balance between a right to 'inner' freedoms to believe and the external freedom to manifest beliefs, which incurs limitations. This is the pattern adopted, for instance, in the Australian State of Victoria, with its Charter of Human Rights and Responsibilities, enacted in 2006.[1] It stresses first the freedom to have or to adopt a religion or belief, and to demonstrate this in 'worship, observance, practice and teaching'. Interestingly there is one article, 14, which specifically insists that 'a person must not be coerced or restrained in a way that limits his or her freedom to have to adopt a religion or belief in worship, observance, practice or teaching'.[2] If people are constrained from choosing their most basic beliefs about the world and their place in it, the free exchange of ideas that is essential for democratic debate becomes impossible.

This is not a hypothetical situation. A state can support a religion by refusing to allow people who have been born into it to give it up. When the tenets of a religion itself opposes 'apostasy', the state appears to have religious sanction for its oppression. One example of this came in 2007 in a widely publicized case heard by the Federal Court of Malaysia, its highest court. The case concerned a convert to Christianity, born a Muslim. She could not have her change of religion officially registered, and hence obtain a marriage licence to marry her Christian fiancé, without an apostasy certificate issued by a *sharia* court. Yet in some Malaysian states apostasy is a criminal offence, and hence even to apply for such a certificate would be to incriminate oneself. The judgment, by a majority of two to one (with the non-Muslim significantly dissenting), rejected her right unilaterally to change her religion. In the words of the Chief Justice, the law clearly stated that the *sharia* court had jurisdiction over cases involving Islam, and thus by necessary implication over matters relating to Muslims renouncing Islam. He held that a person cannot 'at one's whims and fancies renounce or embrace a religion'.[3] Any change had to occur according to the existing laws and practices of the particular religion.

Control of individual belief was viewed as a matter for a religious court, and the highest court in Malaysia was not prepared to override it. The Constitution of Malaysia itself refers to the right of 'every person to profess and practise his religion'. This was not seen by the court as covering a right to change religion, even though human-rights documents insist that it does. Article 18 of the United Nations Declaration of Human Rights upholds the freedom of someone 'to change his religion or belief', although some Muslim countries have always been unhappy about this. The rights of an individual conscience in the Malaysian case are subordinated to the demands of a community. This is in stark contrast to the Western liberal view that sees the conscience of the individual as paramount. Liberals sometimes query the rights and freedoms of religious institutions to set their own standards, when these are seen as oppressive, but it is usually recognized that religious freedom is safeguarded as long as any individual has a right of exit from a religion. This is clearly not allowed in many countries.

Freedom of religion must at its core include the right to leave a religion, and to be converted to another. Even so, if a change of belief is allowed, the question still remains as to which practices are integral to the belief, and how far they will be allowed. The dichotomy between belief and manifestation is a shaky one. The limitations referred to in some human rights documents can be significant. Even if beliefs are allowed, their expression may not be. Limitations referred to in the second section of Article 9 in the European Convention could be potentially far-reaching. The one imposed 'for the protection of the rights and freedoms of others' is particularly relevant when there is a clash between different human rights. There is nothing here to safeguard a right to religious freedom when other rights are brought into play. The Victoria Charter in Australia similarly in its Article 7(2) talks of 'such reasonable limits as can be demonstrably justified in a free and democratic society based on human dignity, equality and freedom'.[4] It does add that the least restrictive means should be used in any limitation, but the words 'dignity' and 'equality' are clearly meant to carry great weight, and could trump religious freedom.

The 'inner' and 'outer' life

The distinction between belief and action, or 'manifestation', can become impossible to draw. How does one know what someone believes if it is never manifested? It becomes an uninteresting truism that people can believe what they like, as long as they never express their beliefs in word or action. This is crucial for those who wish to attack religion. One cannot strike at a belief unless one strikes at behaviour motivated by that belief. Even publicly arguing for a particular position could be seen as behaviour, so, if someone always kept quiet about what he or she really believed, no one would be any the wiser.

The split between private belief and public expression has roots in philosophical views about the character of religious belief. John Locke, in his great *Letter Concerning Toleration,* comments that 'it is in vain for any believer to take up the outward show of another man's profession'.[5] He continues by asserting that 'faith only, and inward sincerity, are the things that procure acceptance with God'. True religion can stem only from an inner 'assurance of faith'.[6] Without that, nothing can be acceptable to God. Locke uses this argument to show that the 'magistrate' can never compel religious belief, or conformity to a particular church. God will never accept what is done through coercion, as opposed to the dictates of conscience.

The argument depends on a distinctively Christian, even Protestant, basis in theology. It emphasizes the importance of the response of the individual believer to God. Membership of a community, and actions in conformity with its conventions, are far from sufficient. This stress on the role of personal faith concentrates on the role of the individual, and this individualism is echoed in the modern approach to human rights. Its historical origins suggest that this stress on the individual is not a neutral view from the standpoint of religion in general. The reluctance of Islam to give priority to the beliefs of an individual over the rights of the community illustrates this. Locke is taking up a definite place in Christian theology, particularly over the question of the nature of the Church. For him, the Church is a voluntary association, 'a free and voluntary society',[7] and he says explicitly that 'nobody is born a member of any church; otherwise the religion of parents would descend unto children'. He thinks this absurd, given his view of the crucial importance of a personal commitment.

Locke places limits on religious toleration. He distinguishes between the importance of freedom in religious matters, and issues concerning the 'public good'. He thinks that, if the magistrate is indeed concerned with the public good, there should not be many occasions when a private person might be required to act against a private conscience. He says explicitly that 'the private judgment of any person concerning a law enacted in political matters, for the public good, does not take away the obligation of that law, nor deserve a dispensation'.[8] He aligns himself with those who would not allow exemptions for conscience, or general accommodation for religion. The law is the law, and it must be obeyed as long as it does not trespass on issues concerning 'worship and ceremonies'. A distinction is drawn between the care of souls, and the political concerns of this life.

When religious belief is described like this, it can easily be seen as essentially personal and private, of no concern to government. Even those who wish to champion religious freedom may be tempted to draw it narrowly, much as Locke does, to include matters of doctrine and ritual, but not matters of morality or politics. The English Court of Appeal tended to see religious freedom in just these narrow terms.

Locke accepts that there has to be civil recognition of ecclesiastical laws, 'and that the subjects of that government both may, and ought to be, kept in strict conformity with that church, by the civil power' but denies that there is any such thing as 'a Christian commonwealth'.[9] He is sometimes seen as advocating the separation of church and state on the American model. For instance, Jean Bethke Elshtain refers to 'his argument against a state church',[10] referring to Locke's view that no man, and no state, can dictate to another in matters of faith, as that has to be an inward disposition. While, as we have seen, his views certainly were to influence the American Founders a century later, it is anachronistic to foist such a view on Locke himself. He was a loyal member of the Established Church of England. He wanted greater toleration for dissenters, and wanted the Church itself to be more tolerant of views within it, so that as many dissenters as possible could be 'comprehended' within it, instead of driven out. In the terminology of the time, he was a 'latitudinarian'. While recognizing the distinct spheres of church and state, he took for granted official recognition of the Church of England.

The distinction between inward belief, on the one hand, and matters concerning the 'public good', on the other, is echoed in modern human rights charters. The contrast between the inner and the outer life, on which doctrines about a free conscience undoubtedly depend, lies at the heart of ideas about a liberal, democratic order. Yet how much should be on the 'belief' side of the line? Matters of ritual and worship take place in the public sphere. If a religion enjoined the regular sacrifice of virgins as part of its worship, this would hardly be part of an absolutely protected area of belief.

All public expressions of faith in worship could be regarded as 'manifestations' of religion, and hence subject to public control. From many religious points of view, the contrast between belief and manifestation is obnoxious. It suggests that, while it may be important to believe what one chooses, beliefs are never of sufficient importance to demand action. Freedom to believe does not translate into freedom to act. Morality is totally independent of religion (itself a distinctive and contentious philosophical position). This suggests that religious freedom makes little difference in the real world. It carries little weight in a choice of way of life. Those who assume that religious liberty consists in the freedom not just to believe certain things, but to act in accordance with those beliefs, are ignored by the dichotomy between belief and manifestation.

In a totalitarian country that tries to stamp out religion as a rival source of authority, it need not matter what people believe, as long as they never admit to it. The state demands outward conformity. An effective way of enforcing control on citizens is to ensure that they share the ideology of the state, and, particularly in education, the resources of the state will try to ensure that. People are always more compliant if they believe in what they are doing. While that is desirable from the point of view of the long-term survival of the regime, all it has to do is to make sure the behaviour of their citizens, and all views expressed, conform with its requirements. No one can know what people really think, if they never admit to it.

This was the situation in much of Communist Europe before the collapse of the various regimes. In Hungary, for example, when a girl criticized Communism at school in the 1980s, her father was summoned by the headmistress, who asked him to tell his daughter to stay quiet. Everyone, it appeared, including the staff, agreed with what she said, but the school could not dare to allow her to say it. It was not her belief that was in question, but her expression of it. This kind of situation is graphically described by Vaclav Havel, who became President of Czechoslovakia, and then the Czech Republic, after the fall of Communism. He stresses that under Communist repression individuals did not have to have certain beliefs, but just behave as though they did, keeping silent about what they themselves thought. He says: 'For this reason, however, they must *live within a lie*. They need not accept the lie. It is enough for them to have accepted their life with it and in it. For by this very fact, individuals confirm the system, fulfil the system, make the system, *are* the system.'[11]

In Czechoslovakia between 1948 and 1989, the legal system enforced a conformity that rested on the first article of the Constitution, concerning the leading role of the Communist Party. People were required to act in their professional lives in ways that could well go against their private beliefs. Judges passed verdicts even when they were against their consciences, and teachers taught beliefs about history, politics, and religion that they often knew were false.

Is sincerity enough?

Beliefs are not enough. They have to be manifested. Mere freedom to hold them is barely freedom at all. At the very least, they have to be manifested in order to be recommended to others. Having a conscience is not enough. One has to be able to act on it. Charters of human rights can allow that beliefs have to be shared, but a narrow view of what counts as a manifestation might still be taken for granted. There is an incentive to view things in this way so that religion is not given what may be seen by some as undue privilege. It can be allowed its own sphere in worship and ritual. Once it impinges on public life, the claims of religious freedom become subject to the social and political priorities of the day. Laws of general application need not give it any special recognition.

The manifestation of belief immediately brings private belief not only into a public context, but also into a communal one. Seeing religion as merely an instance of the exercise of conscience immediately makes all religion personal. Assimilating religion to 'belief' does the same. Yet my own beliefs about what is right or wrong do not constitute a religion. They are moulded by religious teaching, and religious understandings of the dignity of human beings. An exclusive stress on personal belief omits the communal character of religion. Even if, as we have stressed, freedom of religion essentially involves personal commitment, we have to know what we are committing ourselves to.[12] There is an inherited body of alleged truth that the believers share in. Religions are typically bodies of interwoven belief and practice, which we can choose to take on or reject. In so doing, however, we characteristically join an ongoing community of believers with specific traditions and collective understandings with others, or leave such a community. Even the most individualistic of Protestant denominations would talk of a gathered community. They would never imagine religion was a matter of picking which bits of which beliefs I liked most.

Many contemporary understandings of religion see it as an entirely personal matter, discounting the role of any wider community. This is partly because of the contemporary preoccupation with human rights, and results from the history of the idea. Much of the energy in propagating a doctrine of human rights in the later Enlightenment was directed against authoritarian religion, usually in the guise of the Roman Catholic Church. The rights of the individual were proclaimed in a way that deliberately ignored the wider cultural context in which truth could be discovered and shared.

An example of how a jurisdiction can champion individual belief to the exclusion of any idea of the relevance of a wider community came in a case (already briefly mentioned in Chapter 3) that was heard by the Supreme Court of Canada.[13] In the appeal, significantly allowed only by the narrow majority of five to four, the main conclusion was that religious freedom was about individual autonomy. The case was one about a right by Jews to build *succahs* on the balconies of upmarket flats. This was to fulfil the biblically mandated obligation of dwelling in small huts during the nine-day Jewish festival of *Succot*. The allegation was that the building of such huts broke the terms of a contract with co-owners of the flats that similar constructions would not be allowed. Trellis work and satellite dishes had had to be removed, so as to preserve the appearance of the flats.

In order to reconcile competing interests of different flat owners, an offer was made to construct a communal *succah* in the gardens of the flats. This offer was thought reasonable by the Canadian Jewish Congress, but was rejected. The demand for individual *succahs* was not so central to the Jewish faith that all or most Jews agreed. Yet that proved irrelevant for the court, which maintained that 'the State is in no position to be, nor should it become, the arbiter of religious dogma'.[14] The last thing that the court wanted was to rule how important the construction of shelters was for the Jewish faith.

The conclusion of the court undermines any idea of a communal religion. As in its other judgments, it reduces freedom of religion to the notion of personal autonomy.[15] As the court sees it, this means that sincerity of belief is the only test, and a court could feel qualified to test that.[16] The judgment clarifies its meaning by saying unequivocally that 'this understanding is consistent with a personal or subjective conception of freedom of religion, one that is integrally linked with an individual's self-definition and fulfilment, and is a function of personal autonomy and choice, elements which under-gird the right'.[17]

Religious freedom becomes a personal freedom to do what one wishes. Religious practice becomes whatever an individual believer maintains it is. Sincerity is sufficient. In this case the court protected a practice that had a connection with traditional Jewish understandings, although not one shared by many Jews. If, though, a religious practice is created only by individual belief, rather than by communal under-standings, anything can become religious, and the idea of religion as deserving special protection becomes meaningless. In this case, there was an issue whether a contract freely entered into should have been overturned. If the reason was a clash with religious obligation, respect for religion may have tipped the balance. The Canadian Court prefers to put religion in the context of personal choice. Yet a society that sees religious obligations as the product only of an individual conscience is unlikely to give any special place for religion, and will find that it has to place severe limitations on the kinds of conscientious behaviour allowed. People cannot do whatever they choose to believe is right for them. That would lead to anarchy, with little scope for exceptions to general laws.

One of the dissenting judges in the case about *succahs* wanted to add to a test of sincerity the requirement that a belief, and a practice sup-ported by a belief, is grounded in the precepts of a particular religion.[18] He wanted evidence, not just of personal belief, but also of a 'genuine connection between the belief and the person's religion'.[19] His argu-ment was that religious precepts provide a body of 'objectively identi-fiable data' that can be used to determine genuine religious belief, as opposed to idiosyncratic personal choices. He added that, 'by identify-ing with a religion, an individual makes it known that he or she shares a number of precepts with other followers of the religion'.[20] This makes religion a public and social reality, even if it also demands a per-sonal commitment. A court could establish a link between belief and religion as a matter of fact, even without getting involved in any theo-logical issues about the character of the belief.

Secular liberalism feels comfortable with the idea of autonomy, and would rather change the subject from religion to that. It can cope with issues about sincerity, and would rather not have to decide which of a number of strongly held beliefs are religious and deserve protection. Yet there are often differences between specifically religious views and more general issues of conscience. A religion typically makes demands of its adherents. They are believed to be not of their making but are obligations imposed on them. That is very different from a 'subjective' choice made because I feel like it, and imposed it on myself.

Assimilating religion to wider issues of conscience is very common. Sometimes it is made with a view to ensuring that the religious conscience cannot claim any special privileges, and the ground is prepared for refusing any exemptions on grounds of religion. Objections are dismissed as special pleading by groups who do not deserve special attention. The danger is that devaluing a religious conscience results in all claims of conscience being ignored. Other forms of conscience may claim parity with a religious one and want equal respect. The reality is that all then may be equally ignored, if they obstruct favoured social priorities.

Challenges in medicine

Nowhere are the stakes higher than in the domain of medical ethics where matters of life and death are in play. Julian Savulescu, an expert in medical ethics based in Oxford, gives an example of this. He says: 'There is no reason to give preference to religious values over non-religious values per se.'[21] He justifies this with the tendentious assertion that 'religion is about faith: ethics is about reason'.[22] Yet faith can, and should, be highly rational,[23] and too many voices in moral philosophy over the last century have suggested that ethics is not rational. The contemporary acceptance of various forms of moral relativism, sometimes under the influence of postmodernism, is one example of this.[24]

Savulescu argues that medical practitioners should follow the requirements of society, and not their own principles. He firmly says that 'public servants must act in the public interest, not their own'.[25] Further the public interest is to be determined by the law, not by the moral judgements of individuals, or the Church or other institution. The same type of reasoning was used against the civil registrar who did not wish to conduct civil partnership ceremonies. Savulescu generalizes the argument so that it applies in medicine. Those who wish to give priority to their conscience over the demands of society should give up their job. He says: 'A doctor's conscience has little place in the delivery of modern medical care ... If people are not prepared to offer legally permitted, efficient, and beneficial care to a patient because it conflicts with their values, they should not be doctors. Doctors should not offer partial medical services, or partially discharge their obligations to care for their patients.'[26]

Savulescu's specific target is doctors with religious scruples. He argues that 'to treat religious values differently from secular moral values is to discriminate unfairly against the secular, a practice not uncommon in medical ethics'.[27] Yet he also rules out any conscientious objection, however motivated. The role of all in medicine, whether doctors, nurses, pharmacists, or others, is to obey the commands of the state. For Savulescu, 'to be a doctor is to be willing, and able, to offer appropriate medical interventions that are legal, beneficial, desired by the patient, and a part of a just health care system'. Yet what is 'beneficial' may be highly contested, and, if individuals are not allowed to follow their consciences in judging what that is, this raises the prospect of a state being able, for its own reasons, to insist on the most appalling practices. Nazi Germany may be an extreme example, but it is still a salutary one. For Savulescu, 'in public medicine, conscientious objection involves inequity and inefficiency'.[28] Yet the idea that doctors should ignore their professional conscience, to obey whatever are the fashionable pressures of the day, is worrying.

The idea of service to our fellow humans ought to be a central ideal in medicine, and it is commonly rooted in religious beliefs about the intrinsic value of human beings. If human life is seen as sacred, there is a powerful motive for taking up medicine. When confronted with demands for euthanasia, assisted suicide, some forms of genetic engineering, or even abortion, some may object so strongly that they may refuse to participate. If conscience, particularly a religious one, is not respected, doctors and others who entered medicine to save life could find that they have to end it deliberately, or leave their profession.

Savulescu acknowledges that a doctor's values should 'of course' be accommodated if that does not compromise the quality and efficiency of public medicine.[29] That concession seems curious, if such consciences are irrational, and against the public interest. Perhaps he does recognize that conscience can be important, and that individuals suffer if they are not allowed to live by their deepest beliefs. The problem comes when enough object to thwart the implementation of some medical policy. Yet if enough doctors resist to put the provision of a 'service' in doubt, that may say something about the kind of medical procedure it involves. Respect for the judgement of professionals would certainly seem advisable, since that is what the practice of medicine rests on. Laws passed without regard to the views of those who have to implement them may be bad laws.

Not just those with a religious outlook are threatened, but so is anyone prepared to bring a personal moral judgement to bear on what they are required to do. Doctors with any sense of morality, or at least a willingness to make judgements that go against the fashions of the day, need not apply. Freedom of conscience marches with freedom of religion, even if they should not be assimilated. Respect for conscience gains when religion is respected, and loses ground when religion is swept aside. Those with strong religious convictions form the principal target, as they are often the most stubborn. Yet battles for freedom of religion have also brought a wider respect for anyone's right to follow conscience.

Attacking the conscience of medical practitioners when it conflicts with public policy is as menacing as any totalitarian restriction on public manifestations of belief. Both situations indicate the artificiality of separating belief and manifestation. I can believe in the sanctity of life, but could be expected to participate in euthanasia or assist in a suicide. This is little different from believing in the falsity of Communism, perhaps for religious reasons, but being forced to teach its truth in school. Both attack the very roots of human freedom.

Restricting practices

The individualist view of religious belief shown by the Canadian Supreme Court may appear to include too much, by making personal belief its focus, but it might seem to err on the side of toleration. Yet, we have seen that, the wider the scope of a religious conscience (or any conscience), the more restrictions on manifestation are likely to be introduced. An absolute freedom to believe entails restrictions on living in accordance with that belief. Even this freedom to believe, however, could be questioned. May some beliefs be so irrational and obnoxious that it is wrong even to hold them? Many Nazis were perfectly sincere in their beliefs about the 'final solution' and the rightness of racist policies towards Jews. Sincerity in that case, if anything, made the situation worse. It was the beliefs that were abhorrent, and not just the practices that they gave rise to. It may appear an advantage that a court does not have to judge the truth or falsity of any belief, and concentrates on sincerity, but that suggests not just the impartiality of those administering the law, but that the law they are administering itself has no moral basis, and no substantive principles to apply.

No legal code can be so neutral that it is unable to distinguish between good and bad. In particular, it has to decide which manifestations of belief are acceptable and which unacceptable. The limitations prescribed by the European Convention of Human Rights put everything in the context of democracy, but refer to notions of public safety, public order, health, and morals, as well as talking of rights and freedoms. These ideas are all freighted with moral views built up over the centuries. The reference to 'morals' makes it crystal clear that any court, and the European Court in particular, has to stand somewhere. An ever-present danger is that such matters will be decided in accordance with political convenience or fickle public opinion.

One pervasive problem continues to infect the artificial split between right to believe and the conditional right of manifestation. What is the difference between a manifestation of a religious belief, and an accompaniment of it that is not an essential consequence? When a Muslim woman wears a face veil, is that a religious obligation or a cultural phenomenon, to be found only in some Islamic countries? The subjective criterion would say that, if a woman thinks it is a religious obligation, then it is for her, whatever other Muslims might say. An insistence on determining the 'right' Islamic view on this, in the face of different practices, would improperly involve courts in theological controversies that are internal to Islam.

Even if courts do not want to do this, and accept there are religious reasons for wearing such a veil, they must have views of what is and is not acceptable in society. A face veil, as English courts have concluded, can be inappropriate for a teacher in a classroom. Yet any court's conceptions, however tolerant and inclusive, of what makes a well-ordered and even a 'moral' society have to come from somewhere. Some may opt out of such decisions, leaving it to individual choice. As the problems about 'manifestation' indicate, however, once we step from private belief to civil society where beliefs clash, we have to operate with some collective principles. What can be manifested and what cannot? These issues are acute if we believe in the importance of individual freedom, and also in the importance of individuals living by what they believe to be most important. We may believe that religious belief and its practice should be safeguarded. The problem is where to draw the line between religious practices we may not share but must tolerate, and those that cannot be allowed in a democratic society. Democratic values, however, as championed by the European Convention, are not neutral. They themselves have a definite history and foundation.

8

Necessary Limits to Religious Freedom

Should conscience be accommodated?

The distinction between religious belief and its manifestation may be an artificial one, and unacceptable to much religion. That admission does not solve the problem of whether some genuine religious practices should be constrained, or even banned altogether, even in a free and democratic society. However much religion should be protected from the arbitrary power of the state, it has to be recognized that some forms of religion are pathological, and cause great harm, by any normal human standard. They may command child sacrifice, or mass suicide. They can encourage morally contentious behaviour, such as polygamy. No state can allow all religion to go unchecked, even if it should not see all religion as intrinsically harmful and divisive. The problem is what criteria it can draw on to distinguish between acceptable and unacceptable behaviour.

One view would be to assume the truth of one religion, to adopt its standards, and to judge all those who dissent from it as dangerous. Although it is easy to dismiss this as an undoubted attack on personal freedom, and freedom of conscience, some may see what they understand as a wilful refusal to accept the truth as ruinous for everyone. They may feel that, unless society is organized in accord with the will of God (as they see it), it will inevitably fail. There have been times in the history of Christianity when heretics have been hunted down and apostasy punished. The institution of the Inquisition in its various forms enforced standards of belief after the Reformation challenged the unity of the Catholic Church. Coercion could, at the extreme, involve torture, and even the ultimate sanction of death. This was not just a medieval institution, but one that continued to exercise power in parts of Europe until the beginning of the nineteenth century, requiring correct doctrine, stamping out superstition, and looking for heresy. In Catholic Malta, for example, the last Inquisitor did not leave until 1798, when the Inquisition Tribunal was suppressed by the French, during their brief period of control there, as Napoleon was advancing through the Mediterranean.[1] While the contemporary Roman Catholic Church has asked for forgiveness for that part of its history, some Islamic countries are still only too ready to enforce conformity in even harsher ways.

What, however, is wrong with a religion imposing its views on others, particularly if it is thought to be in their interests, perhaps as a means of salvation? Some may think that the appeal to an objective truth encourages intolerance, and an acceptance of relativism can encourage toleration, as there is no longer any all-embracing 'truth' to enforce. Yet this is simplistic, as, without objective moral principles as a restraint, there is nothing to inhibit me or my society from imposing particular views on others. Intolerance of other ways of life can be built into the fabric of a society.

Toleration, respect for others, and ideas of human dignity are wrapped up together. I will respect others' beliefs, not because I do not think it matters what they believe, but because of some ethical obligation to them. Respect comes, not from indifference, but from a positive view that their conscience matters as much as mine, that their freedom is as important as mine. Truth can be the ally of genuine toleration and not its enemy. I have to think other people matter, and religion may teach me that they do. A belief in the truth of a religion need not lead to coercion. It can include the idea that individual freedom is precious, and that, as Locke maintained, God does not value any forced belief. A grip on truth can then provide a firm hold on the importance of religious freedom.

No legal system, however, can shirk the problem of how far the law should accommodate a religious conscience. Some limitations of practice may still be required. It may not be enough, though, that a society disapproves of certain behaviour. The dilemma came to be seen with great clarity in an exceedingly controversial judgment made in the United States by the US Supreme Court in 1990, in the case of *Smith*.[2] The case concerned the use of peyote for religious reasons, despite general criminal prohibition of the use of the drug. Should a legal exception be made? The court's stance was summarized by Justice Scalia when he said: 'Respondents urge us to hold, quite simply, that when otherwise prohibitable conduct is accompanied by religious convictions, not only the convictions but the conduct itself must be free from governmental regulation. We have never held that, and decline to do so now.'[3]

He went on to say that there was no suggestion that Oregon's drug law regulated religious beliefs, their communication, or the raising of one's children in those beliefs. Yet it clearly impinged very directly on certain religious practices, just as the banning of alcohol would on, say, a Christian Mass or Eucharist, demanding the use of wine. Clearly there is at work here the questionable distinction between belief and practice. Freedom of belief is regarded as safeguarded, even if there is little freedom of practice.

Justice Scalia does not want the court to be dragged down the road of judging which practices are important or 'central' to a religion and which are not. Balancing a compelling state interest against the importance to believers of certain practices could lead to that. An alternative would be the Canadian Supreme Court's opinion that the believer's view of the matter is paramount. Sincerity is all that counts. Justice Scalia believes that adopting this test for all actions 'thought to be religiously commanded' would be 'courting anarchy'.[4] Exemptions from the law could be provided because the law conflicts with personal beliefs that the believer, and perhaps no one else, sees as 'religious'. In Europe, where religion is widened into 'religion or belief', the position would be even more intractable.

One leading legal academic, Kent Greenawalt, puts it this way: 'The heart of Justice Scalia's opinion is that courts should not have to decide when religious claims of variant strength should triumph over state interests of variant strength.'[5] The Justice believes that this is a matter for 'the political process'.

Issues about accommodating religions would then be decided by the legislature, and not by judges, giving power to the majority, however composed. Justice Scalia says of the problem of minorities: 'That unavoidable consequence of democratic government must be preferred to a system in which each conscience is a law unto itself or in which judges weigh the social importance of all laws against the centrality of all religious beliefs.'[6] The choice, as he sees it, is between the anarchy of each person being his or her own judge of what is to be religiously important, and handing power to the representatives of the people, even if they are unsympathetic to some minorities.

The judgment in *Smith* proved enormously controversial in the United States, provoked disagreement between Congress and the Supreme Court, and resulted in a plethora of 'Religious Freedom Restoration Acts' in various states. An example is that of Florida, which specified that the government (of the state) should not 'substantially burden' a person's exercise of religion, unless in 'furtherance of a compelling governmental interest'. It should use the 'least restrictive means' of furthering that interest.[7] Similar language was used elsewhere. Matters would often have to proceed on a case-by-case basis, with the courts weighing a 'substantial burden' against 'compelling governmental interest'. The difficulties in doing so are clear, and a simpler approach can appear attractive. As Greenawalt comments: 'if no one provided religious exemptions, no one need worry about sincerity, burden and government interest.'[8] The temptation can be to say that everyone is subject to the same law, and must equally be expected to obey it.

A law that is neutral in its intention may not be neutral in its effects, but may place substantial burdens on those with particular beliefs. An employer being given the discretion as to which days to give as days off may unfairly restrict the ability of Christians to attend public worship on a Sunday (or Jews on a Saturday, or Muslims on a Friday).[9] Yet the law is the same for everyone. In this, and other cases, the view of the European Court is that freedom of religion is adequately safeguarded by the fact of freedom of contract.[10] Freedom of religion, it seems, is guaranteed by the fact that one is always free to be unemployed. That, it might seem, would in American terms certainly be a 'substantial burden'.

In examining 'burdens', courts can trespass on theological ground. Greenawalt asks how judges can possibly determine how substantial a burden is to religious practice. As he says: 'A court must avoid deciding what is *really* important religiously; it cannot tell Roman Catholics that, after all, grape juice is just fine for communion, if they believe wine is essential.'[11] The latter was, of course, a real issue during Prohibition in the last century in the United States. Greenawalt believes that 'courts must take claims as they are sincerely presented by those who seek an exemption'.[12]

Racial versus religious discrimination

The interference of courts in theological issues is not just a continuing problem for Christians. One of the first cases to be decided by the newly established United Kingdom Supreme Court caused great unhappiness among Jews. Separated in October 2009 from the legislature in theory, and in geographical fact, across Parliament Square in London, the former Law Lords are now Justices of the Supreme Court. It will take several years to see whether this new arrangement puts them on a collision course with the will of a parliament, of which they are no longer part, in particular through their enforcement of the European Convention of Human Rights. This particular case did not do that, since it involved the interpretation of parliament's own 1976 Race Relations Act. The court did, however, follow the uneasy precedent of other such courts in controversial cases involving religion, such as those of the United States and Canada, by being almost equally divided in their decision, in this case five to four.

The dispute involved a boy who had been refused admission to an Orthodox Jewish school in London, because he was not recognized by Orthodox standards as Jewish. His mother, Italian by birth, had converted to a branch of Judaism in a manner not recognized by Orthodox Jews. The court was being asked to intervene in an internal theological dispute among different forms of Judaism. Because the child of a Jewish mother is automatically Jewish, through matrilineal descent, it is crucial for Jews to be able to decide whether a mother is authentically Jewish. A mother can become Jewish by conversion, as well as through her own descent, and the official recognition of that conversion by the relevant authorities is important.

The court ruled that in fact, though not in intention, the school had been guilty of direct racial discrimination, on the grounds that its admissions policy depended on 'birth link criteria' and that these led to the boy being treated less favourably on ethnic grounds.[13] The need not to discriminate on racial grounds trumped any consideration of religious freedom. Lord Phillips in his judgment exhibits a certain discomfort about this result, reflecting that the Jewish people should perhaps be allowed to follow their law.[14] He asserts strongly, however, that, 'if such allowance is to be made, it should be made by parliament and not by the courts'.[15]

This highlights two recurring themes in this kind of case. First is the undoubted reluctance of courts, particularly in Europe, to allow apparent discrimination, in the light of a religious, or indeed other, conscience. Yet that itself produces a form of discrimination against religious people, in this case Jews, who are not being allowed to practise the faith they have held for thousands of years, in a manner that has no doubt helped to preserve them. It is ironic that, in this case, this is being done in the name of avoiding racial discrimination. Many have seen discrimination against Jews as a cardinal example of that. Because British legislation absolutely forbids any racial discrimination, religious principles are made to take second place.

The second point echoes the line taken by Justice Scalia in the United States. The issue is whether it is the function of parliament, congress, or other legislatures, to provide exceptions, or accommodation for religious scruples, or whether the courts should be left to deal with these on a case-by-case basis. In the United States, talk of 'substantial burdens' or a 'compelling governmental interest' solves little, but pushes cases back to the courts, as the issues will be so dependent on particular facts. There must always be a role for courts, but there is much to be said for legislatures giving a clear lead and foreseeing difficulties. That is clearly the preference of Lord Phillips.

Legislatures are more genuinely representative, and, in any case, it is very unsatisfactory for important issues to be settled by one vote in a divided court. Even legislatures, however, have at times been unready to provide exemptions on grounds of religion in the face of fierce lobbying by other interest groups. Yet however important race, gender, and so on are as illegitimate grounds of discrimination, the fact remains that discrimination on grounds of religion or belief is equally prohibited, and yet is often overlooked in contemporary legislation, particularly in the United Kingdom, as this case illustrates.

The sense remains that the Supreme Court is intervening in a theological issue beyond its competence. The fact that Lord Phillips's judgment begins with a quotation of four verses of Deuteronomy should set alarm bells ringing. Although an essentially religious question is in dispute, we are told by Lord Kerr, when the answer to that question 'has consequences in the civil law sphere, its legality falls to be examined'. He continues: 'If the decision has consequences that are not permitted under the law, the fact it was taken for a religious purpose will not save it from the condition of illegality.'[16] That is true as far as it goes. Yet it does not solve the question how far a religious motivation deserves accommodation in the first place. There is reluctance to grant exceptions to a law on religious grounds, particularly when forms of discrimination are in question. Yet the result can be discrimination on grounds of religion.

The dissenting judges saw things rather differently. Lord Hope says that 'it has long been understood that it is not the business of the courts to intervene in matters of religion'.[17] He quotes an earlier judgment to the effect that 'religion is something to be encouraged but it is not the business of government'.[18] The attitude of the European Court of Human Rights is rather different, since it holds that the state must remain neutral, and, presumably, avoid 'encouraging' religion. That has not been, until now, the British approach. In this case, issues of admission to a school, and the alleged racial discrimination, were matters for civil law. Yet as Lord Rodger points out, the issue was not the mother's race, but that she had not converted to Judaism under Orthodox auspices.[19] The dispute was about her conversion, and we are back with theology.

Lord Rodger's conclusion is that 'the decision of the majority means that there can be in future no Jewish faith schools which give preference to children because they are Jewish according to Jewish religious law and belief'.[20] He muses that 'the majority's decision leads to such extraordinary results, and produces such manifest discrimination against Jewish schools in comparison with other faith schools that one can't help feeling that something has gone wrong'.[21] One thing that has certainly gone wrong has been the court's willingness to wade into a theological dispute without any willingness to appreciate its nuances. One obstacle may have been the way in which the Jewish position on ethnicity based on matrilineal descent was out of line with the beliefs of other religions. In particular, Protestant assumptions about the importance of individual religious commitment still influence many secular assumptions about individual freedom, even though that is unacknowledged. There is always a temptation to universalize such beliefs, and to fail to appreciate differences in other religions. The court significantly remarks that, 'as far as we know, no other faith schools in this country adopt descent-based criteria for admission'.[22] This demonstrates an intrinsic inability of any court to deliver informed judgments about the theology of faiths appearing before it, particularly if they are alien to the personal experiences of the judges. US jurisprudence has always been exceedingly wary of such 'entanglement'.

Churches and the law

Issues of religious freedom do not just impinge on individuals, since the beliefs and practices of religious institutions, as such, can come into conflict with more secular priorities. As with individuals, the mere fact that something is done in the name of religion does not mean that it can be justified. Even the idea that churches can be allowed to regulate themselves, and exercise their own discipline, has been called into question in the first decade of the twenty-first century in many countries because of a continuing series of scandals about alleged child abuse by Roman Catholic priests. The reluctance to hand over priests to the normal processes of law even though their activities might often have been criminal suggested a desire to protect the reputation of the church at all costs. The idea of 'the freedom of the church' can be abused, in ways that damage the vulnerable.

The opposite approach of making the Roman Catholic Church conform to secular laws, perhaps concerning non-discrimination, also causes problems. In the United Kingdom, and the United States, Catholic adoption agencies have had to close down their activities, rather than go against Roman Catholic doctrine and place children for adoption by gay couples. A valuable service to society has thereby been lost. One English High Court judge found at least a prima facie case in the suggestion that the withdrawal of the service by one such agency meant that adoptive parents were no longer found 'for a significant number of children who would otherwise go unprovided for'.[23] That argument would not satisfy those who believe that the principle of non-discrimination against gay couples is of overriding importance, no matter what the calculation about the social effects of any withdrawal of the service by a Catholic agency. In fact, it did not suffice to protect Catholic adoption agencies. Any idea of accommodating a Catholic conscience was ruled out by the Charity Commission, even though same-sex couples could still adopt children through other agencies.

In this argument, the principle of religious freedom was disregarded. It was dismissed with the view that 'religious belief (in the form of the tenets of the Roman Catholic Church) could not possibly justify the

denial of Catholic Care's adoption agency services to same-sex couples, since it was a manifestation of non-core beliefs'.[24] Further it took
place in an essentially public sphere, 'being both funded in part by, and
carried out in part on behalf of, a public authority'.[25] There we have
several dangerous assumptions. First, we again encounter confident
assertions about what are and are not 'core' beliefs, with the idea of a
core being presumably drawn to the most narrow points of doctrine.
Manifestations of other beliefs, particularly those with ethical implications, can then be dismissed. The fact that the Roman Catholic Bishop
of Leeds himself had asserted to a previous tribunal that beliefs about
marriage were core should have given everyone pause for thought, as
the judge himself recognised.[26]

Second, there is the idea that publicly funded operations should be
conducted without any sensitivity to religious scruples. It is taken for
granted that religion is a matter of private beliefs, without relevance to
public life. Third, it appeared to follow, according to this line of thinking, not only that religion has no role in public policy, but that public
policy can ruthlessly pursue its own priorities without taking note of
religious scruples. Religion, it seems, has no rights in public life, not
even the limited right to be respected, and accommodated.

The idea that religious organizations should be wholly subject to
the demands of the civil law reflects the increasing indifference of
many to religion. The contrasting idea that religion should be encouraged has, in many eyes, to be rejected, on the grounds that it does not
warrant special privileges. The law is the law, it seems, and should be
applied impartially to all, no matter what individual, or collective, burdens ensue in particular cases. Yet this is to ignore the special claim of
religious freedom. If the institutions of any religion are, without hesi-
tation or any weighing of the effects made, subject to the demands of
the law, whatever their own doctrines, secular interests are bound to
come to dominate those of a religious nature.

Another example, from the European Court of Human Rights,
showed the unwillingness of the court to give weight to the doctrines
of a church, as against the rights of individuals. An organist in a Catholic
parish in Germany was dismissed when he was found to be having an
extramarital affair with a woman who was expecting his child. This
was against Catholic teaching, but the court found for him on the
ground that these matters were at the heart of the applicant's private
life.[27] The right to respect for privacy trumped any right a religious

institution had to demand that its employees (particularly one involved in public worship) live by its principles. This demand for equal respect, and recognition of equal dignity, ensures that institutions have little say, even in ensuring that their teaching is observed by their own employees. The result is that there is no respect for the particular ethos of a church or other religious institution, and indifference as to whether a religion can continue to uphold its principles through example and teaching. The institution, the court believes, has no claim on someone's private life. An employment relation, at least of someone who is not ordained, which is based on civil law, cannot be given some ecclesiastical status. It cannot be 'clericalized'.[28]

Considerations of equality again come to the fore. Let us take the example of the equality of men and women, and their need for equal treatment. This would be regarded a bedrock principle in any modern democracy. The Roman Catholic Church does not agree with the ordination of women priests, and it can still be a contentious issue in other denominations. The law does not look kindly on employers who discriminate deliberately against women. Should the Roman Catholic Church be treated any differently? This is not an easy issue, since many would agree that there are some forms of treatment of women that cannot be tolerated by the law, even if they may have the sanction of some religion. In addition to polygamy, which we shall shortly consider, other practices, such as forced marriages, make women subservient, and might appear unacceptable. Once again, we have to know where to draw the line. One writer asks whether, given the same principle of upholding sexual equality, we should prohibit any church from refusing to ordain women. He says of this: 'It seems that we have taken our concept of sex equality as a non-negotiable condition of group accommodation and, at the same time, taken another fundamental right—religious freedom—and just eliminated it from the equation.'[29] His point is that the harm of imposing our views of equality on a group contrary to its religion 'is discounted completely by those who would prevent the harm of sexual inequality'.[30]

Freedom for churches?

Just as insidious as the direct confrontation between issues of religious freedom and other rights is the chipping-away of the right of church and religious organizations to be in control of their own affairs. Employment law in some jurisdictions is now going beyond organists and reaching clergy. Traditionally churches have been able to operate their own disciplinary procedures against clergy and normally expect a higher standard of behaviour of them than would operate in the secular sphere of employment. In Britain, clergy have been seen by law as 'office-holders' and not subject to a normal contract of employment. With the growth of statutory protection for employees, the issue has arisen whether employment arrangements between a church and its ministers are subject to the civil law.

One case, which received little public attention, nevertheless symbolized a sea change in attitudes to the role of churches in employment.[31] A minister could no longer be regarded as a 'servant of God' and thus acting in an area beyond the reach of the civil courts. The minister in question was from the Church of Scotland and was alleging sex discrimination in her treatment in a disciplinary matter. The House of Lords maintained that she had 'rights and duties defined by her contract, not by the office to which she was appointed'.[32] It dealt with a Directive from the European Union, asserting that 'the principle of equality which lies at the heart of the Equal Treatment Directive is of general application'.[33] Since the Church of Scotland ordains women on the same basis as men, it has to accept this, and was not allowed to claim that the Directive did not include its jurisdiction over ministers.

One commentary on the case notes: 'One of the few points of law decided unanimously in *Percy* seems to be that, in matters of discrimination law, the constitutional status of the Church of Scotland offers it no special protection.'[34] A minister may feel he or she has been unfairly treated by a church hierarchy, and legislation about various forms of equality provide many opportunities for church practice and the rights of an employee to come into conflict. Statutory rights are not regarded as a spiritual matter, but as a matter of civil contract enforceable in the courts. In Scotland, it has often been argued that the Church of Scotland and the state are 'separate and distinct',[35] in contrast with the closer relation of the Church of England to the apparatus of the state. Yet, as this case shows, the sphere of the Kirk (the Church of Scotland) is being considerably narrowed. As always, the issue is not which side is correct in its judgements, but that the Kirk is not being given the freedom to order itself in a way it chooses. The standards by which it has to be governed, and the exercise of clergy discipline, may no longer be its own.

The Church of Scotland has in the past seen great battles about the role of the civil courts and their jurisdiction over the ecclesiastical sphere. Presbyterians have always been sensitive about the encroaching power of the state on the rights of the Kirk. It traced these to the Act of Union of 1707 between England and Scotland. One controversy, concerning the jurisdiction of civil courts over the church, even provoked the 'Disruption', the splintering of the Presbyterian Church in Scotland in 1843, when a third of the Church of Scotland literally walked out. They marched out of the General Assembly, meeting in St Andrew's (now St Andrew's and St George's), the elegant Georgian church in Edinburgh's New Town. The result was the building of rival churches round Scotland, forming the 'Free Church of Scotland'. That adjective 'Free' says it all, since they were not subject to the interference of the state in their affairs. The Church of Scotland Act of 1921 was intended to secure the position of the Church of Scotland as the 'national' church, but one free of the interference of the state in its affairs. This led to the reunion of the main components of the Presbyterian Church.[36]

In a comment on the *Percy* case, linking it with the 'Disruption', Lord Rodger, himself now a Justice of the United Kingdom Supreme Court, says that 'the simple fact is that a civil court will be reluctant to accept that it cannot deal with what it sees as an allegation of a substantial wrong'.[37] The *Percy* case provoked none of the uproar that led to the Disruption. Yet, as Lord Rodger suggests, it raises 'that self-same vexed question of the spiritual independence of the Church of Scotland which...split the Church and Scottish society at the Disruption in 1843'.[38]

As societies become more aggressively secular, civil and religious standards may increasingly diverge. Has religion then any rights to be accommodated, or must it acquiesce in what it believes to be wrong? A striking example where both individual behaviour and the customs of a religion seem unacceptable in a modern society lies in issues concerning polygamy. This was outlawed in the nineteenth century in the United States, when it was practised by Mormons, and there are still some religious communes in North America that appear to practise it illegally. A greater challenge to Western ideas of monogamy comes from some Muslim elements, which see no reason why their own religiously sanctioned marriage practices should not be sanctioned in Western countries. The British government has come perilously close to recognizing polygamy by giving social security payments for more than one wife, when several wives are brought from overseas.

Polygamy seems to many to involve the exploitation of women. Some, though, cast doubt on whether it should be outlawed. The American philosopher Martha Nussbaum suggests (presumably from a contemporary feminist standpoint) that Mormon polygamy in the nineteenth century was no worse for women than monogamy, as then practised. She concludes that, given the standard of a governmental compelling interest that, 'if there were a sex-equal polygamy practiced on genuine religious grounds, there is no very strong argument for its invalidation.'[39] This might seem an inevitable, but unwelcome, result of paying notice to the importance of religious practices, as against the general law of the land. Once, it will be said, exceptions are made, we are on a slippery slope, leading not just to the legal recognition of polygamy, but to the fragmentation of the law.

Many would hold that the idea of a 'sex-equal' system of polygamy itself strains credulity. Can women really flourish is such circumstances? The undoubted fact that polygamy can be religiously sanctioned may not excuse it, if it can be shown, on any reasonable basis, to be harmful to women and to wider society. However much weight should be given religious freedom, it would be difficult to argue that it can itself trump every consideration, any more than it should always be trumped. This is particularly so when the individual rights of members of a religious community, such as women, appear to be trampled on by that community, or when the wider well-being of a society, including children, may be put at risk. Polygamy may suit the interests of some men, but that does not answer the moral question of what enables most people to flourish or what constitutes the common good.[40] Even from a theological point of view, it could be argued that religious injunctions cannot issue from a loving God, if they visibly increase human harm.

Reasonable accommodation?

Religious freedom should not be ignored, but cannot sweep aside all other considerations. How then can we decide? The American willingness to balance governmental interests against burdens on those who are religious leads inexorably to judging each situation case by case. There is still the problem of deciding how weighty an interest must be or how substantial a burden. Nevertheless the principle is established by such a method that religious freedom itself matters, and that religion deserves accommodation when this possible.

This was underlined by the report of a commission set up in the Canadian Province of Quebec to look at the accommodation of cultural differences. Religion loomed large, and the Commission linked the issue with that of equality in the face of an increasingly diverse society. It claimed that, 'little by little, the law has come to recognize that the rule of equality sometimes demands differential treatment'.[41] Its argument is that respect for diversity inevitably involves a process of accommodation, as opposed to one side dominating the other. It was concerned with the effects of 'indirect discrimination', whereby a neutral law would bear down more severely on some than on others because of the cultural and religious practices. A non-religious example it gave was of a reasonable rule forbidding students from having syringes, which could bear down severely on those with diabetes. There are many examples in the religious sphere, not least connected with dress, where similar considerations apply.

The Quebec Commission advocated what it termed 'reasonable accommodation'. The question is often what precisely is reasonable, and a position of neutrality concerning all principles will not help. We have to decide what counts as a pressing need, or an overriding interest. The alternative is to see society as simply the ground of warring factions with conflicting interests, who have all to be bought off. There must be some vision of what makes a just society and what constitutes human good and harm. Nevertheless, the idea of reasonable accommodation highlights the need to adjust rules when they bear down unfairly on some categories, including religious believers.

The Commission traced the need to accommodate religious practices (and other cultural practices) to the idea of equality itself. Instead of seeing equality and for religious freedom as being in conflict, it claimed that equality demands respect for religion. This is all part of what it sees as 'a greater respect for diversity' and the need to manage coexistence 'based on an ideal of intercultural harmonization'.[42] Different beliefs require equal consideration. The Commission argued that 'the duty of accommodation created by law does not require that a regulation or statute be abrogated but only that its discriminatory effects be mitigated'.[43] It gave as an example allowing Jews and Muslims to celebrate their religious holidays, in the same way as 'Catholics, who, almost without exception, have always had permission to be absent from work on Sunday, Christmas Day, and at Easter'.[44] It maintained that 'it is the rule of equality or fairness that prevails: what is legitimate for one faith is legitimate for the others'.[45]

How far, though, can religious believers stray from the norms of the society of which they are members and still demand 'reasonable' accommodation? Any society has to take a stand on basic beliefs that are seen to constitute the society. Multicultural tolerance can easily collapse into relativism. The approach of the Commission raises questions, but legislation does need to be accommodated to particular circumstances, if it is not to bear unfairly to a greater degree on some than on others. A right to equality, it seems, should, in the words of the Commission, be implemented in a way that 'is more attentive to the diversity of situations and individuals'.[46]

The Commission wanted to adhere to a principle of secularism, which upholds the neutrality of the state to all religion and non-religion. What it termed the 'moral equality of persons', combined with 'freedom of conscience and religion', together, according to the Commission, express the basic purpose of secularism.[47] It is unclear how these values can be promulgated from a position of neutrality, since moral equality (not to mention freedom) is a substantive notion itself requiring justification. The Commission suggested that the display of the crucifix in the Quebec National Assembly had no place in a secular state.[48] That proposal was instantly rebuffed by the Assembly, and the challenge is how to hold on to the beliefs and traditions of a people while being open to, and being willing to accommodate, those who have a very different worldview. Do the requirements of equality, and the demands of freedom, involve giving up the traditions that have made a people what they are? That is an unresolved issue in Quebec, as in many other places.

9

The Challenge of Equality

Is equality more than impartiality?

Equality is a crucial element in justice, which entails equal treatment under the law. The blindfolded figure of Justice (*Justitia*) with her scales shows that justice is no respecter of persons. Yet it is absurd for justice not only to refuse to favour people, but also ideas, beliefs, or principles. The idea of justice is far from being emptied of all moral content, and cannot risk undermining its own validity. Plato, in his *Republic*, saw it as one of the most fundamental of objective moral principles, albeit one that was often challenged or cynically manipulated. If the idea of equality were to demand the equal treatment of all beliefs, without commitment to any, the status of justice as a moral principle, able to withstand the abuse of power, would be undermined. Those who see the state as being essentially neutral about all beliefs must equally respect the view of Plato's opponents in ancient Athens, and their contemporary equivalents, that justice is just the 'interest of the stronger'. Yet that is to ride roughshod over the idea of equality before the law, a principle referred to in the British context by Lord Bingham, an eminent British judge, as 'a cornerstone of our society'.[1] It is a principle that has not always been put into practice, as can be seen when we reflect on the categories of people who have not been regarded as fully equal.

Many have incurred legal disabilities, and have not been able to hold public office because of their beliefs. As Lord Bingham points out: 'It is a regrettable fact that British law not only tolerated but imposed disabilities on Roman Catholics, Dissenters and Jews not rationally based on their religious beliefs, and disabilities on women not rationally connected with any aspect of their gender.'[2] At the time, reasons were given for the lack of toleration, and even John Locke was reluctant, while advocating general toleration, to tolerate Catholics, because they delivered themselves 'to the protection and service of another prince'.[3] Given the threat in England under James II of the establishment of a centralized, Catholic regime on the French model, Locke's fear of Catholic oppression was all too reasonable. He had to face the perennial problem of how far one should tolerate the intolerant.[4]

The Constitution of the United States, a century after John Locke had been writing, set itself firmly against any religious tests, proclaiming, in its Article VI, that 'no religious test shall ever be required as qualification to any office or public trust under the United States'. All should be treated as equal. Current conceptions of equality, however, go beyond the crucial idea of equality under the law. In Quebec the idea of reasonable accommodation was intended to meet perceived cases of indirect discrimination, where the consequences of a law were more burdensome to some than others. As the Quebec Commission maintained, the effects of a strict application of a norm could impinge 'on a citizen's right to equality'.[5] This reasoning closely connects discrimination, even if 'indirect', and a loss of equal status. The formal equality of equal treatment under the law is then seen as insufficient, and as itself the cause of injustice. A general law may bear down more hardly on a group with particular religious beliefs.

A Canadian case illustrates this.[6] An apparently harmless law of general application in Alberta, requiring photographs on driving licences, caused grave problems for Hutterian Brethren, a small religious community, which believed that photographs broke the Second Commandment (against the making of images and likenesses). They were, therefore, unable to drive without going against their beliefs. A narrow majority (four to three) of the Canadian Supreme Court concluded that the requirement, which was mainly to prevent identity theft, was justified, and that the Hutterites had to accept that their beliefs carried with them some costs to themselves. One of the dissenting judges, however, said that the inability for members of an isolated community to drive in rural Alberta meant that 'the photo requirement was not a proportionate limitation of the religious rights at stake'.[7] As in many such cases, the issues will be dependent on particular facts. Given that general laws can never anticipate every burden imposed, the Canadian Chief Justice says that, when there have to be limits on religious practices, 'the seriousness of a particular limit must be judged on a case-by-case basis'.[8] The issue in this case was just how great were the burdens being imposed.

The argument about photographs could arise in the first place only because it was agreed that equal treatment was not enough. Equality of treatment can produce considerable inequality in outcome, with burdens that may be unjust being placed on some precisely because of their religious beliefs. 'Equality', thus seen, can be linked with the idea of disadvantage, so that, if some are perceived as labouring under particular handicaps, they are judged to be less equal in their society. They do not have the same opportunities as others, and, in the name of equality, they can seem to deserve special treatment, perhaps in the form of legal exemptions, to redress the disadvantages they suffer.

This idea of disadvantage can, however, be carried much further, with a wish to use the law to redress disadvantages that are not just the creation of law, as they were in the Canadian case. Muslim women, for example, might be identified as a disadvantaged group, which deserves special attention. This can provide a motive for 'positive' discrimination, which deliberately picks groups for more favourable treatment, to remedy perceived inequality. The problem is that this is the mirror image of the discrimination that marks some group, on racial or other somewhat arbitrary rounds, and ill treats its members for that reason. In both cases, individuals are being picked out and treated, either well or badly, not for their own qualities but because they are part of some wider whole, however defined.

The injustice of this is clear when discrimination is to people's detriment. Does the same objection hold when some are picked out for favourable treatment? Resentment can grow among those who feel that they are themselves being penalized because they are not members of the favoured group. Social unrest in Quebec, in the face of attempts to accommodate immigrant communities, led to the setting-up of the Commission already referred to. The pursuit of some forms of equality can quickly lead to social engineering in ways that arouse antagonism.

How important is 'disadvantage'?

The idea of accommodation itself trades on that of disadvantage, and takes us away from the simple idea of equality under the law. The law, it seems, can acquire its favourites. Facially neutral laws can bear down more on some than on others, sometimes because of their religious beliefs, and exemptions provided. Once, though, 'disadvantage' is identified as an important feature in the drive to equality, minorities are going to get more attention than majorities. The laws in a democracy are passed by majorities, and they will not need protection from themselves. There seems an inexorable process in the pursuit of equality, whereby minorities gain more attention than majorities, particularly through legal appeals to human rights. This happens in the case of religion, when minority religions in a given society can obtain more attention than a perceived 'majority' religion. The paradox is that, in increasingly secular societies in Europe, all forms of religion are minorities at the mercy of the democratic process. Even so, Christianity may find itself struggling at times to receive the same respect, and attention, as the minority religions of immigrant communities.

The idea of disadvantage is used in regulations in the United Kingdom concerning discrimination on grounds of religion or belief. The relevant clauses concerning discrimination refer to a practice applied to person B when it applies equally to other persons not of the same religion or belief. Indirect discrimination occurs, as was quoted by the Court of Appeal in London, if this 'puts or would put persons of the same religion or belief as B at a particular disadvantage compared with other persons'.[9] It is clear that the idea of disadvantage is applied to a group, and not just individuals. The particular case in question concerned an employee of British Airways who was stopped from wearing a small silver cross on a necklace. Although this aroused such public debate that British Airways changed its policy, the Court of Appeal still found against her, and it was suggested that members of other religions would have been treated more favourably.

The idea of disadvantage loomed large, but the court claimed that it had received no evidence that Christians as such had been placed at a disadvantage, since, as the previous tribunal had heard, visible display of the cross was not a 'requirement of the Christian faith'.[10] Once again we find a court thinking it can pronounce on what is important for Christians. Most Christians do not see the need to wear a cross, but some do, as the prime symbol of Christianity. While this is a personal choice, being told one cannot wear it begins to introduce further considerations. Is one being told to hide one's faith?

The rule may have been one about jewellery, but more was at stake. The court ends its judgment by saying that the case illustrates problems that arise when an individual or group asserts that a practice adopted by an employee 'conflicts with beliefs they hold but which may not only not be shared but may be opposed by others in the workforce'.[11] The court suggests that in such circumstances a blanket ban may be the only fair solution. That, however, raises the spectre of those antagonistic to religion having a veto on any manifestation of religion. If there is conflict, it seems, this should be resolved by religious people being compelled to hide their beliefs

As in other cases, the idea of belief was so circumscribed that attitudes and behaviour resulting from religious beliefs can be regarded as independent of them. In a case concerning the suitability for fostering children of a Christian couple who have traditional beliefs about the immorality of homosexual practices, the same distinction was made between their religious beliefs and attitudes associated with them. Anyone without religious beliefs, but with similar views about homosexuality, would have been treated in the same way by a local authority, and the couple could not prove indirect discrimination against their religious beliefs. The High Court in London said: 'If the defendant's treatment is the result of the claimants' expressed antipathy, objection to, or disapproval of homosexuality and same-sex relationships, it is clear . . . that it would not be because of their religious belief.'[12] They were not, it seems, being treated less favourably than others in a similar position. Yet this conclusion was reached only by discounting the role their religion played in their lives. If religion was blotted out of the picture, then of course they were not discriminated against on grounds of religion.

Equal believers or equal beliefs?

Attempts to accommodate religious beliefs by making exceptions to the law may be justified in the name of equality, on the grounds of redressing disadvantage. Yet they go against the idea that the law applies to all equally. Even framing laws with exceptions built into them in the first places cannot deal with all possible problems. The Canadian Chief Justice says: 'By their very nature laws of general application are not tailored to the needs of individual claimants.'[13] If, though, a majority refuses to deal with the burdens placed on minorities, there will be a tug between the ideal of equality under the law, and that of equality as the product of dealing with disadvantage.

When equality becomes our sole aim, we may be tempted into all kinds of social intervention to achieve a more equal society. As Marxists once found in their pursuit of economic equality, attempts to do so involve challenges to freedom. Social engineers are liable to think that more legal intervention, and more regulation, will achieve their goals. Equality is by no means the same as 'equal freedom'. Achieving equality for some by restricting the freedom of others needs justification. Treating all religions in the same way is not the same as allowing everyone equal freedom of religion. The idea of non-discrimination between religions is so pervasive that at times it seems to constitute what is meant by freedom of religion, so that the state has to be neutral between all religious stances. Yet the state may wish to protect freedom of religion just because it has a specific view of the importance of freedom, which some religions may wish to challenge. We have seen how some religious belief can rule out the possibility of conversion to another religion. No country should take a neutral view about the worth of such beliefs.

It is crucial in conceptions of human rights that people be given equal respect as human beings, with an equal, intrinsic dignity. A Norwegian philosopher claims that 'the normative foundation of the entire edifice of modern human rights is the public doctrine of inherent dignity'.[14] All then have an equal right to exercise their freedom to believe what they wish, but that, as we have seen, could never mean that the content of their beliefs has equal value. Some would even want to deny the idea of our intrinsic dignity.

The idea of equality and non-discrimination is also constantly put forward as the cornerstone of all human rights. Another writer says that 'equal treatment and non-discrimination has been identified as a fundamental directive of the legal idea: that is, the most basic norm which ought to guide the conduct of persons in political authority and be embodied in the laws of the state'.[15] He concludes that any 'state-imposed arrangement that would prefer one religion over the other' would involve such illegitimate discrimination. He holds that 'freedom of religion may never be exercised in a manner that would violate human dignity'.[16] His conclusion is that 'countries founded on libertarian principles which permit freedom of religion or belief to trump individual rights founded on human dignity and equality are at odds with international standards of human rights protection'.[17] The examples he gives are those of female genital mutilation and racial segregation, both of which have claimed some form of religious sanction.

Some religion has sanctioned, and does sanction, practices that go against basic moral principles, because they inhibit full human flourishing. Both the practices mentioned involve the use of power by some to the detriment of others. We can catalogue many other abuses that have been cloaked with the support of some religious view. Suicide bombers manifest a twisted view of their religion, but claim a religious inspiration for what they do. Similarly, the imposition of the death penalty for apostates may be a terrible onslaught on the idea of freedom of religion, but it can occur in the name of a religious principle. No one doubts that horrendous things can be done in the name of some religion or other. It is one reason why religion, and religious practices, of all kinds should be subject to public rational scrutiny, and not thought a matter of only private concern.

Such cases should be distinguished from terrible cases—for example, in child abuse—where followers of a religion, even priests, have simply failed to live up to the principles their church proclaims. Hypocrisy—and, in theological terms, 'sin'—is one thing. We are then operating within the ambit of one religion and applying its principles. When, though, we wish to condemn the practices of a religion, or of some of its adherents, from the standpoint of external principles they would not pretend to hold, things are more complicated. We can point to what constitutes human flourishing, and insist on the importance of equal dignity. Yet these are contested issues. What one religion regards as unacceptable because it devalues women another may feel is part of the natural order of things.

Does 'equality' replace religion?

Secular thinking, caught up with issues concerning equality and non-discrimination, treats its own views as superior to those of any religion. It will not brook the invocation of religious freedom in order to defend what it regards as discriminatory practices, whether against women or any other group. 'Equality' and 'non-discrimination' are seen as so crucially important that, as principles, they have to override religious freedom in every case. The language of equality, non-discrimination, and human rights in general fills the vacuum left, at least in Europe, by the decay of institutional Christianity. It can be proclaimed with the kind of dogmatism associated with the worst elements of religion, with little appeal to reason or justification.

Yet important concepts such as human dignity and equality should not just be asserted, but have to be part of a justifiable worldview. Saying that they are the bedrock of democracy does not take us much further, since all too many in the contemporary world are contemptuous of 'Western' democracy. There needs to be justification for assuming that the demands of equality not only cannot be trumped by those of freedom of religion, but in practice seem to be trumps themselves. When equality and freedom clash, freedom seems to lose. So far from there being no hierarchy of rights, as is often asserted, in practice the right to religious freedom seems well down any list of priorities.

Freedom of religion has been attenuated into freedom of 'religion or belief', and all too often it seems to become merely a part of freedom of conscience. The result is that, with the inherently subjective associations of 'conscience', it cannot be allowed to get in the way of the alleged objective status of the rights and the dignity of humans. These, it seems, cannot themselves be seen as the happy deliverances of individual consciences, but have to form the framework of the society in which consciences can be allowed to operate. Yet objective truths have to be established somehow, and we have to understand why they are true. They cannot be so merely because it is convenient for society, or even essential for its future.

Human rights law, however laudable its intentions, does not always sit easily with the tradition of law that has grown over the centuries through custom and precedent in common law jurisdictions. Inevitably the existence of legally enforceable documents concerning human rights gives considerable power to the courts, of the kind we have seen exercised. Curiously, there was no explicit legal right to free expression, or freedom of religion in Britain before the European Convention on Human Rights was given legal effect by the 1998 Human Rights Act. That did not mean that there was severe constraint on any right to freedom of speech, before the state magnanimously recognized it as enshrined in law, any more than that people were not free to practise a religion before the state explicitly granted that freedom. As the eminent judge Lord Bingham says: 'in practice everyone was free to write and say whatever they wished provided it was not forbidden.'[18] In other words, the basic starting point was individual freedom, which could be restricted if the state considered there was good reason, as in cases of slander and libel. Freedom was the default position before we got into the clutches of the law.

The culture of rights can make it appear that rights are conferred. We hold a right to our freedom in so far as the state allows us. The state can also then decide that some rights are more important than others, so that our freedom can be overridden. Instead of us being free to do whatever is not prohibited, we are free only to act according to rights conferred. The default option is then that we do not have permission to act unless expressly allowed to do so. If we are seen to challenge the equality of others, as defined by the state, we are not given the freedom to do so.

Seeing rights as conferred by the state, or by international agreements, is not the only way of looking at them. It is not the American way, as witnessed by the phrases from the Declaration of Independence, 'that all men are created equal' and that 'they are endowed by their creator with certain inalienable rights'. The Declaration echoes the phrases adopted the previous month by Virginia in its Bill of Rights, the first section of which refers to 'certain inherent rights, of which, when they enter into a state of society, they cannot, by any compact, deprive or divest their posterity'. Such 'natural rights', as adumbrated by John Locke, act as a check on governments, and cannot be their creation. The fact of inalienability stems from their relation to the will of God, an inalienability that, Locke believed, would be hard for an atheist to make sense of. Jeremy Waldron comments, in the context of Locke's views, that, if an atheist cannot make sense of that, 'he cannot grasp the point that a certain sort of respect is due to each one of God's creatures *as such*'.[19] In that case, the atheist will find it difficult to lay hold of the idea of human equality, without any idea of humans as God's workmanship.

If human rights are only the creation of governments, they can be manipulated by any government as appropriate. Rights function only if they can be seen as built into the scheme of things in ways that are recognized, but not constructed or destroyed by human whim. When seen as beyond the reach of government, our freedom and equality cannot be arbitrarily ranked for its convenience. Both are fundamental features of what it is to be human.

Equal liberty sometimes creates paradoxes, with the needs of freedom and those of equality pulling in opposite directions. However, one cannot cancel the other out. People may misuse their freedom and fail to respect others as equal. Demands for equal treatment can involve restrictions on people's freedom to act. Once, though, we regard both freedom and equality as being bound up with what it is to be human, pursuing one at the expense of the other has to be ruled out. There must be a balance, however difficult to achieve in individual cases. We are back with the idea of reasonable accommodation, albeit an idea that does not see social disadvantage as the major determinant.

Children's rights

The drive to equality has swept aside the artificial barriers, which allowed discrimination against whole groups. Yet one class of people should not perhaps be recognized as possessing that freedom. Any egalitarian social theory, looking at the rights of all, has to look at the situation of children. The cry of 'children's rights' is often heard. If we are serious about equality, and think that in any political community all are equal, where does that leave children? They are human and, presumably, of equal importance with adults. Should they therefore be treated in the same way? In the case of religion, should they be subject to what may be seen as the prejudices of others—namely, their parents?

Professor Richard Dawkins, in his widely read attack on religion *The God Delusion*, treats a religious upbringing as a form of 'child abuse', going so far as to suggest that bringing a child up as Catholic inflicts more psychological damage than sexual abuse.[20] While this might be a rather colourful exaggeration, he goes on to complain that our society 'has accepted the preposterous idea that it is normal and right to indoctrinate tiny children in the religion of their parents, and to slap religious labels on them—"Catholic child", "Protestant child", "Jewish child", "Muslim child", etc., although no other comparable labels: no conservative children, no liberal children, no Republican children, no Democrat children'.[21] His point is, presumably, that beliefs should not be imposed, but should be adopted knowingly and voluntarily. This may be more apposite for some religions than others. As we have seen, a child is born Jewish, according to Jewish belief, while Christians, particularly Protestants, would be much more likely to stress the importance of personal belief and commitment. In this, Dawkins is reflecting his own upbringing in showing a Protestant bias in his view of religion.

There is, though, a serious point at issue. Should children be specifically brought up in a particular faith? Dawkins says: 'Let children learn about different faiths, let them notice their incompatibility, and let them draw their own conclusions about the consequences of that incompatibility.'[22] He thinks they should be left to make up their own minds, when they are old enough, 'about whether any are "valid"'.[23] This is similar to the liberal view of how religion should be taught, if at all, in schools. It lay behind the objection of the European Court of Human Rights to the perceived privileging of the teaching of Christianity in Norwegian schools. Yet the way Dawkins puts the case shows how such an approach can veer from neutrality into contempt for all religion, and may even be motivated by it. Religions contradict each other, and cannot all be right, and so it is implied that very likely none of them is. The way he puts 'valid' in inverted commas, and does not even allow the possibility of a religion being true, suggests how easily the message can be conveyed that no religion could be rationally adopted.

A liberal approach to the idea of public reason, as evidenced in the work of John Rawls, wishes to distinguish between public standards of justification, and private beliefs that citizens may happen to have.[24] Religion then becomes particularly vulnerable, because of its controversial nature. One writer, however, takes this approach further. He says: 'The claim I want to defend is that the idea of public reason should be extended so that it constrains *parental* conduct, as well as the conduct of politicians, judges, public officials, and citizens.'[25] He extends the idea of what is public into the heart of the family, so that parents should not impose views on their children that cannot be justified by the standards of 'public reason'. Otherwise, a child's autonomy is not respected.

Yet even a liberal recognizes that a child has to be brought up believing in the need to respect others. Where do such beliefs come from? We are told by the same writer that 'a sense of embeddedness within a liberal culture can supply a raft of commitments and convictions, relating to the freedom and equality of individuals, a related conception of social cooperation, and of the norms that constrain individual conduct which flow from these ideas'.[26] Freedom and equality, it seems, are part of our liberal culture, and that is all that needs to be said. Yet these ideas have been the achievement of centuries, and arose against a very specific historical background. The idea that they are not just as controversial as the religious beliefs out of which they may well have grown is highly optimistic. We cannot take it for granted that our children will love freedom or respect equality if left to their own devices.

Indeed, if we really believe that some beliefs are important for human flourishing, it would be perverse not to want to pass them on to our children. This applies to beliefs about freedom, and it applies with equal force to beliefs about what may be regarded as most important in life—namely, religious ones.

A liberal approach should want children to learn to think critically and to understand the reasons for beliefs they hold. If children do not learn from their parents, they will learn, as they may do anyway, from the many influences, prejudices, and fashions of the wider society. Parents must reflect whether that is likely to be any better than the guidance they can give. Certainly, children cannot learn in a vacuum how to be rational. They cannot be critical, without anything to be critical about. Everyone has to start from somewhere. Indeed, as we saw at the beginning, it is very likely that we are born with a natural inclination towards certain kinds of beliefs. It is not just 'indoctrination' that inclines children to see the world in ways conducive to religion.

Granting premature autonomy to children can be dangerous. They must be taught to value freedom, and freedom can properly and responsibly be exercised only if it is guided by reason. Rationality itself is a capacity that we gradually learn to exercise as we grow. In the meantime, parents can only guide children in the ways they themselves think best. They can do no other, a fact itself recognized by the United Nations Universal Declaration of Human Rights. The third section of Article 26 asserts that 'parents have a prior right to choose the kind of education that shall be given to their children'. Any policy that regards children as having the freedom of adults to choose their religion gives them a responsibility they are not old enough to bear. It assumes that they have skills of critical reasoning that they have still to acquire.

IO

The Foundations of Equality and Freedom

How is democracy grounded?

Freedom and equality are often treated as if they are self-evident principles, governing our politics and morality. Yet most people in most parts of the world at most times have not been treated as free and equal. Deep springs of yearning in human nature can be tapped, and the suggestion that all ought to be free and equal produces an eager response in those who are downtrodden. Yet what are the principles of freedom and equality built on? The fact that 'we', in the twenty-first century, organize our democracies on that basis does not provide sufficient grounding. It is mere sociological commentary on a situation that could change.

Democracy is bound up with beliefs in both freedom and equality, but that is not a defence of any way of life, but merely a description of it. A commitment to equality rests on an uncertain foundation, not least because there are so many different views about what is meant by equality. Treating everybody of equal worth, and deserving equal respect under the law, is not the same as striving for greater social and economic equality. The role of freedom is also vulnerable if it is not rooted in anything beyond the contingent fact that we (whoever 'we' are) happen to value it. Once religion, in various forms, can appear a threat, or just loses its influence, freedom of religion can appear of little count, instead of being a prime, if not *the* prime, example of a free conscience at work. We have to have some idea about why such freedom matters. The roots of religion in human nature can, as we have seen, suggest that human flourishing demands the free exercise of such basic impulses. That insight, however, needs to be embedded in a coherent view of the world and the place of humans in it. Just because we want freedom, and even need it, there must still be an argument as to why all humans should be given it. This is particularly so if we are free ourselves. Why do other human beings matter, even if they are at the other side of the world and cannot adversely affect us?

Western countries want to uphold democracy and its 'values'. The status of such values is unclear, and it can appear that they are just what happens to be valued at the present time. The beliefs and principles that produced them are ignored. Yet in the modern era democracy arose in Christian countries, and it was founded on specifically Christian principles concerning individual freedom. Even in ancient times Athenian democracy was a very limited form of democracy, restricted to male citizens, cutting out not just women, but the slaves on which the society depended. Some will point out the autocratic tendencies of the Roman Catholic Church through the centuries, and suggest that its conversion to ideas of religious freedom is very recent (most specifically in the Second Vatican Council). For that reason, modern democracy took root first in Protestant countries, but it was inspired by Christian principles. Its achievement was gradual, but in both Britain and America democracy could not have attained its present form without a Christian underpinning. It was perhaps significant that American theologians were influential in helping to change Catholic ideas about religious freedom at the Second Vatican Council.

In England, church and state, religion and society, have been entwined since Saxon times. Christianity has formed its very identity as a nation, and its character as a democracy. In the United States, there may have been a greater institutional distance between church and state, but the underpinning of Christianity for the character of its people, and the nature of its institutions and laws, has always been strong. No one saw this more clearly than Alexis de Tocqueville, who some sixty years after the foundation of the American Republic was struck by the intertwining of religious principle and American democracy. He said: 'I do not know whether all Americans have a sincere faith in their religion, for who can search the human heart? But I am certain that they hold it to be indispensable to the maintenance of republican institutions.'[1] He goes on to say: 'The Americans combine the notions of Christianity and liberty so intimately in their minds, that it is impossible to make them conceive the one without the other.'[2]

Much of his analysis depends on the insight that the conduct of a democracy must depend on what its citizens are like. They must learn how to use their freedom responsibly. Democracy is not just founded on religious principles, but needs religion to teach its citizens how to act in the wider interest, as well as for their own good. The decay of institutions, such as churches, intermediate between state and individual, means that the power of the state will increase to fill the vacuum. There is no other context left in which individuals can be influenced so as to act for the interests of others as well as themselves. Tocqueville saw the danger of a people unconstrained by anything but their own will. He asked: 'What can be done with a people which is its own master, if it be not submissive to the Divinity?'[3] He also saw the connection between religion and human nature. He did not know about the cognitive science of religion, but that did not prevent him from coming to similar conclusions, asserting that 'faith is the only permanent state of mankind'. He says that 'if we only consider religious institutions in a purely human point of view...they belong to one of the constituent principles of human nature'.[4]

Tocqueville was echoing the beliefs of the Founders of the United States. They had varying ideas of the right connection between religion and the state, and Thomas Jefferson was more radical than most, with his undoubted anti-clericalism, and bias towards a 'rational', Unitarian, faith.[5] Even he saw that belief in freedom rested on a theological premiss. He argued that we are answerable for the 'rights of conscience' only to our God.[6]

A genetic fallacy?

Some would resist the conclusion that, because the Founders of the United States had certain principles, that means that the Constitution they drew up can depend only on those principles. Similar arguments would be provided in other countries with an avowedly Christian heritage. Just because certain democratic principles evolved out of a certain context, does that mean that democracy still needs that context? Even if some brands of Christianity promoted democracy, does democracy depend on Christianity?

The same issue can arise in the context of science. There is good reason to see science as having arisen from a specifically theistic, if not

Christian, context. It gave grounding to a belief in an intelligible, ordered world, structured according to the mind of the Creator.[7] Does that mean that science can receive ultimate justification only in a theistic context? In each context, some deny that, just because a certain set of beliefs produced modern ideas about science, or democracy, science and democracy need those ideas for their continued justification. The ideas, it seems, can float free and exist independently. Alfred Stepan, for instance, in an article on democracy and religion, talks of what he termed 'the fallacy of "unique founding conditions"'. He asserts: 'This fallacy involves the assumption that the unique constellation of specific conditions that were present at the birth of such phenomena as electoral democracy, a relatively independent civil society, or the spirit of capitalism, must be present in all cases if they are to thrive.'[8]

In a strict philosophical sense, this observation must be true. What gives rise to a belief can be very different from the justifying conditions for the belief.[9] To think otherwise is to commit what has been termed the 'genetic fallacy'.[10] Once beliefs and ideas are merely related to their background instead of being examined on their merits, truth becomes inaccessible, and relativism beckons. We look at why people came to the beliefs they did rather than whether the beliefs are valid. Yet Christian principles played more than a causal role in the establishment of democracy and ideas of freedom. They formed a basis for their justification. If so, how far can the ideas be sustained without that justification? An alternative one must be produced, or there is a risk that people's commitment to freedom wanes as the reason for it is forgotten.

Is faith irrational?

The idea that Christian principles can continue to give life, and support, to basic political and legal principles is anathema to many. It runs against the caricature of blind 'faith' depending on neither reason nor evidence, and without the resources to exercise any power of rational persuasion in the public square. This picture is even given explicit warrant in the courts, as a reason why religious principles, so far from underpinning public life, may not even deserve public respect. That appeared to be the basic message given by Lord Justice Laws in remarks made during the course of a judgment in the Court of Appeal in

London. They received wide publicity. Indeed, the *Washington Post* even reported them under the byline 'Can anyone save religion in England?'[11] The context of the remarks was refusal of leave to appeal for an applicant who was a paid counsellor, but wished to be exempted from any obligation to work with same-sex couples in issues of psycho-sexual therapy. He lost his job because of Christian principles that, he claimed, stopped him from doing this, and one might also wonder whether he would have the relevant expertise. He was regarded as guilty by his employer of 'gross misconduct' because he refused to comply with the employer's equal opportunities policy. That seemed to uphold the rights of homosexuals, but not those of religious believers, and successive Employment Tribunals agreed, following the earlier *Ladele* judgment, previously discussed in Chapter 6.

Lord Justice Laws argued against the idea 'that the courts ought to be more sympathetic to the substance of the Christian beliefs referred to them than appears to be the case, and should be readier than they are to uphold and defend them'.[12] In fact, that could not be the issue here. Courts should impartially administer the law, not enter into theological judgments about the worth of particular views. Nevertheless, the fact that particular views are strongly and sincerely held by someone ought not to be ignored by the court, and, in the name of religious freedom, accommodated if possible. This is not to uphold a particular belief, but to respect the right of a person to manifest it as he or she sees fit. That is built into human rights documents. It is to be balanced against other rights, and not overridden as a matter of course. Lord Justice Laws acknowledges the 'vigorous protection of the common law and Article 9 of the European Convention of Human Rights of the right to hold and express religious beliefs', but then points out that this does not mean they offer protection to the content of beliefs.[13]

That is not the problem in this case. No one suggested that the appellant was demanding that his views be adopted by everyone, or that the law should implement them. That would be an extraordinary position, and irrelevant to the issue of religious freedom. What is at issue is the right of someone with strong religious beliefs to be allowed to follow them, regardless of what others think. Can such beliefs be accommodated, when a policy opposed to them is being pursued? The disagreement is not about who gets his or her way in a democracy, but about how far minority views should be accommodated.

Lord Justice Laws, however, seems so concerned about the danger of what he terms 'theocracy' (which he thinks is 'of necessity autocratic') that he maintains that 'the precepts of any one religion—any belief system—cannot, by force of their religious origins, sound any louder in the general law than the precepts of any other'.[14] From a position that insists on impartiality towards individuals, he has jumped to the idea that religious principles are irrelevant even to the underpinning of law. The law is neutral, so neutral, it seems, that it cannot be influenced by particular religious principles, nor can it bring itself to regard religion as worthy of any special accommodation.

The reason he feels able to do so is that, in a fairly brief paragraph, he has taken up a highly contentious position in the philosophy of religion. Whether it is the function of any court to get involved in such philosophical issues is another matter. He argues that conferring 'any legal protection or preference upon a particular substantive moral position on the ground only that it is espoused by the adherents of a particular faith... is deeply unprincipled'.[15] Yet giving such legal protection may not be to agree with the position but to recognize it is strongly and sincerely held. If we believe in religious freedom, we may think the law should, if possible, protect such positions, particularly when we do not share them.

Lord Justice Laws, however, makes sweeping observations on the nature of religion as such. He says that 'in the eye of everyone save the religious believer religious faith is necessarily subjective, being incommunicable by any kind of proof or evidence'.[16] It follows, he says, that it cannot be justified for a law to be promulgated to protect a position held purely on religious grounds. To do so, he provocatively says, is 'irrational, as preferring the subjective over the objective'.[17] He muddies the waters by conceding that a religious belief may be 'true', even though not 'objective'.[18] While the idea of objectivity is a slippery one, contrasting it with the subjectivity of belief normally suggests a link with the idea of truth, just as 'subjectivity' suggests that appearance is everything and truth is not in play. However, even if religious belief were to be seen as subjective, in a strong sense, there could be a case for respecting and accommodating it, on the grounds that it matters greatly to individuals. Even so, the allegation that religion is necessarily subjective, without recourse to proof or evidence, is highly contentious.[19] The whole tradition of natural theology argues otherwise.

Further, the notion that 'faith' has no validity apart from the commitment of its adherents, and is not an ally of reason, goes against the self-understanding of many religions, especially Christianity. Lord Justice Laws has swept aside centuries of Christian theology, and taken sides in a complicated philosophical debate about the relation of faith and reason, which has echoed down the centuries, and is as live today as ever. Moreover, he has made assertions that are totally unsupported by argument. His views may echo common assumptions in contemporary society, but that does not constitute a coherent position in the philosophy of religion.

The idea that religion cannot be rationally based, rationally argued for, and rationally criticized is a pernicious one. It results in the exclusion of religion from public affairs, removing any beneficial influence it could have, and also allowing its worst aspects to fester away from the public gaze, free from any challenge. It also removes the ability of any religion to give support to fundamental legal principles. Since the English common law has been shot through with Christian assumptions from its origins, that must be a difficulty. Law and religion have always been closely entwined in England. Lord Justice Laws, however, will have no truck with giving Christianity any special place. No religion can be allowed to be more influential than any other. If, he says, using a familiar argument, the precepts of any one religion sound any louder in the general law than any other, 'those out in the cold would be less than citizens'.[20]

The credibility of religious belief, it seems, is undermined because of its alleged intrinsic irrationality. The content of any given belief cannot be protected 'in the name only of its religious credentials'.[21] The fact that a belief is religious in character may actually count against it when one person's belief is weighed against another's rights. Instead of religion deserving attention and accommodation, brisk assertions have dismissed the relevance of religion in underwriting law, or in deserving any special legal recognition. Referring to the *Ladele* case, the judge says that 'there is no more room here than there was there for any balancing exercise in the name of proportionality'.[22] As in *Ladele*, any idea of freedom of religious practice is thrust aside in preference for the need not to discriminate on other grounds, in this case sexual orientation. The right to manifest religious belief was not overruled by a more pressing right. It does not seem to have been allowed into the scales in the first place.

Rights without religion?

Other jurisdictions take a more positive view of religion and the need for religious accommodation. The United States Supreme Court was faced with a long-running dispute about the display of a cross in a remote area in California, as a war memorial to the soldiers fallen in the First World War. As so often happens, in controversial cases concerning religion, the final judgment was a close one, five to four. The problem was that the cross had originally been on federal land, and the display of the cross could have appeared to give government endorsement of a particular religion. To avoid this, the US Congress had sponsored a complicated arrangement whereby that particular piece of land was transferred out of public ownership, while the cross was on it. The allegation was that this was in effect a fudge, which implied endorsement and approval of the cross as a 'national war memorial'.

The Supreme Court plurality was motivated by a recognition of the desire of Congress to make 'accommodation' for the beliefs of those who had erected the cross.[23] One can respect beliefs, and the fact that they are strongly held, without implying that one agrees with them. The essence of religious freedom is that people are allowed to follow their religion, even if it is a different one from that of the majority. The accommodation of minority beliefs is what distinguishes democracy from a totalitarian state. The paradox, in the case of the cross, is that it represents the beliefs of the great majority of Americans, and it might appear that the majority are being robbed of rights that should be held by any minority.

What about the more substantive question raised by the curious remarks of Lord Justice Laws, separating law very firmly from any contamination by religion? With his distrust of 'theocracy', he proclaims that 'the State, if its people are to be free, has the burdensome duty of thinking for itself'.[24] Religious principles must not inform its decisions. The state is then the ultimate authority, and appears to operate in a vacuum, seeing no authority beyond itself. The higher authority of God has often been invoked against what could be an incipient totalitarianism. In the United Kingdom, the power of the sovereign, however devolved through parliament, has always been seen as explicitly subservient to God. The Coronation Service sets this out very clearly, putting forward a vision that, if lost, would seem by default to give the state absolute power.

Many would limit the power of the state, while avoiding any reference to God, simply by appealing to a body of explicit rights, to be interpreted by the courts. With the European Court of Human Rights in Strasbourg, Europe as a whole, even beyond the European Union, also sees itself as bound by abstract principles of human rights. In countries that, in Eastern Europe, have so recently suffered totalitarian government, this can be a salutary experience. Many no doubt see it as a practical way of establishing the principles of democracy and of freedom. Yet the problem remains whether this appeal to human rights make sense in Europe or North America without the centuries of Christian tradition, which made human beings appear of supreme importance.

The American philosopher Nicholas Wolterstorff has portrayed the situation well towards the end of his book on *Justice*. He summarizes his argument when he says that, 'if God loves ... each and every human being equally and permanently, then natural human rights inhere in the worth bestowed on human beings by that love'.[25] He concludes that 'natural human rights are what respect for that worth requires.'[26] Elsewhere he writes that 'the recognition of natural human rights is a gift of the Hebrew and Christian Scriptures'. He explains this by saying that, 'once one affirmed that each human being has the worth that ensues upon being created by God and being redemptively loved by God, the recognition of natural human rights is right there in front of us'.[27]

Human dignity

No one can answer the question of the importance, and the validity, of human rights without being willing to adopt some view of human nature and why humans matter.[28] Why are human rights so important? Some would suggest that giving preference to human beings over animals is an example of a 'speciesism' as iniquitous as racism. We cannot take it for granted that humans are uniquely important. We have referred to talk in this context of human 'dignity'. This signals some inherent quality, but we have to give substantive content to the notion.

Saying that others have dignity just because we do respect them is insufficient. For this reason, Martha Nussbaum must be wrong when she maintains that 'dignity probably cannot be defined altogether independently of respect'.[29] Human dignity may entail that we ought to respect everyone equally, and, as Nussbaum says, 'because of that dignity, are to be treated with equal respect by laws and institutions'.[30] To imply, however, that people have dignity because we respect them fails to teach us the grounds of that respect.

Nussbaum goes further and argues that 'the political realm should avoid a comprehensive religious or metaphysical account of human equality, precisely in order to leave room for, and show respect for, the many ways in which citizens interpret this idea'.[31] Unfortunately, interpretations of equality can become so various and idiosyncratic that we lose grip of the idea. Equality, like freedom, is one of the ideas that has, to a large extent, to be non-negotiable, in the sense that all are equal in the sight of the law, and that the law should as far as possible respect their freedom, particularly their freedom of conscience. Yet 'respect' can encourage diversity as an end in itself, and we find ourselves having to respect those who have no room for equality, and are contemptuous of another's freedom. Respect for divergent views takes precedence over any idea of truth. Yet we are then left with no reason ourselves to respect the views of others. Not doing so is as good as doing so.

Many contemporary philosophers would recognize the need to fill out the idea of human dignity to give us some grounding. For instance, James Griffin, in writing about human rights, admits that 'a satisfactory account of human rights must contain some adumbration of that exceedingly vague term "human dignity"…in its role as a ground for human rights'.[32] Griffin, like many philosophers, looks to the idea of personhood as crucial, 'specifically our capacity to choose and to pursue our conception of a worthwhile life'.[33] Yet, as he later admits, 'human rights, on the personhood account, are not universal in the class of human beings: they are restricted to the sub-class of normative agents'.[34]

That must be true for some rights. Children are not in a position to claim the same freedom of religion, or indeed of conscience, that an adult can. The exercise of some rights may involve capacities that not all humans have, but defining dignity in terms of those capacities is dangerous. A liberal would stress the importance of rational consent. Yet are we to believe that people with impaired capacities, as well as children whose capacities are undeveloped, do not bear some rights, or have no 'dignity'? Some basic rights, such as the right to life itself, do not depend on the possession of a particular faculty. It depends on who we are, not on what we can do. Otherwise, some people, like some animals, may be seen as ultimately disposable, even if it is argued that it is in their own interests.

Given that not all have the relevant capacities, grounding worth in capacities restricts the idea of dignity, and hence of worth, in a way that Christian teaching, for example, would find intolerable. From a Christian point of view, all humans—whether ordinary little children, those who have had had impaired mental capacities from birth, or Alzheimer's patients—have worth, because, as Wolterstorff says, they are equally loved by God. Human rights, to make any sense, must be seen as making unqualified and universal claims about the intrinsic worth of all humans. Once qualifications are built into the idea of such rights, we are on the slippery slope to denying rights to whole classes of human beings, even women or those of other races, on the alleged grounds that they do not possess certain capacities. The doctrine of human rights has then been turned upside down, and is proving what it was meant to exclude.

Human rights must be grounded in a full-blooded doctrine of human nature, showing what it is about all humans that warrants respect. Making human autonomy a touchstone fails to explain why many human autonomous choices can be unacceptable. It fails to make the metaphysical case that humans have that kind of rational autonomy in the first place. Traditional Christian (and Jewish) teaching, as Wolterstorff has indicated, has grounded the unique character of humans in the fact that they are made in the image of God, and partially reflect His nature, with the ability to be responsible for rational, moral choices. Griffin is one of many philosophers who readily accept that the modern discourse of human rights is inspired by Christianity, particularly since the Reformation. He says that 'at its core is the idea that human beings are unique, that we are made in God's image (Genesis 1:27), that we too are creators—creators of ourselves, and by our actions, of part of the world around us, on which we shall be judged'.[35]

Can any idea of the inherent dignity of all human beings, together with concomitant rights, survive the removal of the very beliefs that gave them life? If, as Nietzsche's puts it, 'God is dead',[36] can we any longer see everyone as the children of God, and go on respecting them all equally? It may then be difficult to see the importance of preserving freedom of conscience, so that everyone equally can put their core beliefs into practice? Reference to Nietzsche makes the point, as his attacks on Christianity were also attacks on human equality. He deliberately referred to 'higher and lower men',[37] and attacked the possibility of a rational self, as the agent of free choice. His philosophy drew out remorselessly the consequences of a nihilism, which he saw as issuing from atheism, and which he eagerly embraced. The traditional categories of philosophy, such as freedom, rationality, and truth, were called into question. As, more recently, 'postmodernists' have come to see,[38] the whole Enlightenment project, of which the belief in human rights is a notable part, lies in ruins once ideas of reason and objective truth have been removed. We are left with traditional perspectives, and ways of looking at things, with no possibility of giving any of them some overarching justification.

The importance of conscience

If humans can be free and rational, what we believe matters, and how we choose to act matters. We have a choice of which beliefs to adopt. That is why our conception of human nature is crucial. Are we the kind of beings that can make rational choices, and make judgements about we think is true? In that case, those judgements are of inestimable importance. If we are free by nature, we must respect the free choices of others, especially when we disagree with them. If we are sure we live in the kind of world that has been made so that human freedom is valuable, perhaps because that is God's will, we will have no difficulty in accepting this. If, though, we are not sure about the kind of world we live in, or whether there is a God, our very doubt should ensure that we should respect the various choices others make. We are in no position to say that they are wrong.

The only people, it would seem, who can consistently refuse to recognize the freedom of others, or to respect their consciences, are those who not only are arrogantly sure they are right, but also have beliefs about the world that suggest that human freedom is of no account, or does not exist. It will be more important to have the right beliefs than to have adopted them freely. It does not follow that those who believe in objective truth must want to force their beliefs on others. They may see it as true that humans have been endowed with an intrinsic freedom of conscience that has to be respected. That is certainly a Christian belief, and is why Christianity should always be a champion of individual, and institutional, freedom.

All deserve equal respect, but that does not mean that everyone's beliefs are equally sensible. All have freedom, but we cannot all be free to do whatever we like, regardless of others. The perpetual problem will be to decide where exactly to draw the line between acceptable and unacceptable manifestations of belief. This is where protecting the rights of others can be made to appear of paramount importance, and a reason for restricting freedom of conscience. The need to resist discrimination of various kinds can override the apparent claims of conscience. Courts seem to have no difficulty in allowing equality to trump freedom.

Yet democracies are built on the idea of the importance and worth of each person's judgement. They ought to respect religion, because of its deep roots in human nature. When people wish to act according to their conscience, there are particular reasons, to do with freedom, and, indeed, the role of religion in human life, to respect their judgements. Public policy may dictate that their views are not followed, but that should not automatically mean that they cannot be accommodated. Legislatures should be willing to consider exemptions in laws for those who cannot conscientiously follow them, and courts should be more ready to respect religious views, when people find they cannot in conscience follow some practice demanded of them, say in their employment.

Religion and human rights are not opposed to each other. Ideas about human rights owe their origin particularly to Christianity, and religious freedom is itself a prominent right. No charter of rights has ever omitted the right to such freedom, but it is often overlooked, or overruled in the pursuit of other rights. Religious freedom may not be 'the first freedom', and many would hold that there is no hierarchy of rights. If that is so, then all rights matter, and have to be balanced against each other. Religious freedom is, however, certainly not secondary to other rights. Rights to equality cannot trump those to religious freedom. We may then have to decide on a case-by-case basis, with the presumption that the principle of reasonable accommodation should be to the fore.

The right to religious freedom, including the freedom to deny all religion, must be cherished, because such freedom matters. Religious freedom cannot be pushed to one side, because of a disapproval of religion, or some forms of it. Some may see religion as intrinsically divisive and harmful, but they cannot impose their views on others without denying the very right to freedom of conscience that they themselves are exercising. Some say that religious freedom is a species of freedom of conscience. This underestimates the importance of religion in helping to form answers of the most fundamental questions about the place of humans in the world. Even so, it does underscore the fact that freedom of conscience itself is crucial in any list of rights.

As humans, we cannot recognize the role of rights, and our concomitant responsibility in respecting them, without a 'conscience'. Unless we are truly free to judge what is of exceptional importance in how we treat others, we are not exercising one of the most crucial capacities constituting our common humanity. Judgements of equality themselves depend on the rational reflection that constitutes conscience. They are often highly influenced by forms of religion, and conscientious judgement is often a manifestation of religion. Respecting the equality of all needs freedom to recognize the real nature of human beings. Without the possibility of a genuine freedom of religion, and of conscience, there may be no real and lasting commitment to that equality.

Conclusion

Religious freedom as a human right

The single-minded pursuit of equality can lead to the neglect of other basic principles. The ideology of the later Enlightenment saw human rights as independent of religion, and intrinsically opposed to its influence. That is alien to the longer tradition of natural rights stemming from the seventeenth century in England, which influenced the Founders of the United States. For the latter, reason was not essentially secular, but grounded in a theistic understanding of the world. As Jefferson's Bill for Establishing Religious Freedom in Virginia put it: 'Almighty God hath created the mind free.'[1] Rationality and freedom march together. The one cannot be exercised without the other, and both are the result of God's dispensation.

All human rights charters, and national constitutions, as we have seen, include a clause about the importance, not just of freedom of conscience, but of freedom of religion. Religious liberty is not contrary to human rights, but an integral part of our understanding of what human rights are. Many would argue that it is crucial for all freedom. Without the ability to decide, and live by, what we consider to be most important and valuable in human life, we cannot be free. Equality is built into the idea of democracy, but freedom, even the freedom to stand against the demands of the state, is at least as fundamental.

Religion points to an alternative, and higher, source of authority than the state. This makes it vulnerable, and all the more worthy of protection. The exaltation of the state, even if it is made to appear 'the will of the people', can crush the individual conscience. It is worrying that public policy objectives, however worthy, such as the need to stamp out discrimination and promote equality, can in many countries be given the force of law in a way that enforces a secular orthodoxy.

British courts, from the Supreme Court down, consistently refuse to accommodate religious belief, in the face of the demands of equality. This is more than a mistaken view about a hierarchy of rights, with religious freedom not given due weight. Judges make questionable assertions about the epistemological status of religion, and its place in the constitution of the United Kingdom. In the case, referred to in Chapter 9, about the suitability of a Christian couple to be foster parents, their attitudes to homosexuality almost became a side issue. The two judges in the High Court in London quoted with approval the views, discussed in the previous chapter, of Lord Justice Laws about the irrationality and subjectivity of religious belief, and went on to make large claims about the place of religion in England.

They began by making what they regarded as 'an obvious point' that 'we live in this country in a democratic and pluralistic society, in a secular state and not a theocracy'.[2] Although these two are often thought to be the alternatives, there is a great deal of space between a 'theocracy', where there is no religious freedom and domination by one religion or hierarchy (as in contemporary Iran), and a 'secular state', where religion is thought to be a private, and 'subjective' affair. The two are not the only possibilities. The judges set great store by the fact that 'we are secular judges serving a multi-cultural community of many faiths', judging without 'fear or favour'.[3] They also made sociological comments about the fact that 'there have been enormous changes in the social and religious life of our country over the last century'.[4] Yet this essential neutrality in a varied population, with everyone equal in the sight of the law, is different from a secular neutrality inspiring the content of law. The judges quickly passed from the difficulties of administering law in 'a multi-cultural community of many faiths' to major conclusions about the intrinsic character of English law.

The administration of law requires different criteria, in the interests of justice, from those needed by legislators. Judges should be neutral about those appearing before them, but how can laws be neutral? Since laws make distinctions between what is and is not to be allowed, they are never neutral. The only question is what principles inspire them. For these two judges (Lord Justice Munby and Mr Justice Beatson), 'the laws and usages of the realm do not include Christianity, in whatever form'.[5] They say that 'the aphorism that Christianity is part of the common law of England is mere rhetoric'. Yet there seems to be confusion here. It is no function of the law to favour Christians or implement Christian doctrine. That would be to give inequitable treatment to those of other faiths appearing in court. Does that mean, though, that England is a secular state where Christianity has, and should have, no influence on the making and upholding of laws, or the principles implemented by them? Do judicial impartiality and neutrality entail a neutrality to all religious views by the state? The history of England suggests otherwise.

When the common law and Christianity are coupled, the idea is not that the common law favours Christians, but that Christian principles have always given English law its grounding. Basic ideas, such as justice and mercy, stem from theological ideas, so that the law has to answer to higher authority. Principles built into the fabric of democracy have been rooted in Christianity, and the contemporary question must be how far they will survive in any country once their traditional grounding is repudiated. They will be belittled if judges dismiss such views as purely 'subjective', not based on reason.

Freedom and state neutrality

Those who champion the idea of a secular state, neutral to all religion, and see this as a precondition of religious freedom have to spell out the idea of the secularism they espouse. There are many secularisms, some avowedly anti-religious. It is a conceit that secularism generates a religiously neutral state. No state can be wholly neutral about the behaviour it encourages or discourages, and it needs principles to guide it. It is at least arguable that Western secularism, when not simple anticlericalism, was drawn from a distinctively Protestant view of human beings. The idea of the importance, and dignity, of the individual, on which much human-rights law depends, took root on Protestant soil. Even the idea of religious freedom has been largely a Protestant construction. John Locke's philosophy of toleration, with his stress on individual belief and commitment, bore particular fruit in the United States. Yet it was the result of the distinctively Protestant theology in the seventeenth century of such thinkers as the Cambridge Platonists.[6] Modern secularism in the Western world unconsciously universalizes the stress on the individual made by Protestant Christianity but with the religion subtracted. Whether this is a viable and enduring enterprise remains to be seen.

The fact that a secular state is far from neutral (and perhaps cannot be) is seen in the English judges' own rulings. They enforce a particular moral outlook, privileging equality at the expense of freedom of belief and practice. One extreme reaction to the ruling about the fostering of children by Christians with unfashionable beliefs about the morality of homosexual practices was that we were witnessing here a modern, secular Inquisition, imposing through law 'orthodox' standards of belief and practice, in a way that bears down on individual conscience.[7]

The Inquisition in Europe has already been referred to in Chapter 8. It was not abolished in Spain until 1834. Although some of the more lurid punishments had long since been phased out, it remained an effective instrument of social control. Its influence is summed up by a remark in a history of the Inquisition in Malta. We are told that 'most Maltese dreaded the day they would have to face the Inquisition Tribunal'. They were afraid, not so much of harsh sentences, but of 'becoming dishonoured'.[8] There was an attempt to control not only behaviour but belief, and the purpose of resorting to torture in its early days was to extort the innermost convictions of its victims.

In contrast, modern human rights law is supposed to protect belief, and conscience, but the pursuit of equality and of the avoidance of discrimination is leading courts in different jurisdictions to fail to respect the apparent dictates of conscience, when they are in conflict with public policy. Gradually, those who, particularly for religious reasons, find they cannot accept the latest secular orthodoxy come to feel the full force of the law constraining, not only their actions, but the public expression of their beliefs. They are not, it seems, even allowed to talk to children about them. Religious views become denigrated as 'subjective', and the actions that are seen to manifest such beliefs are defined so narrowly as to exclude most forms of public behaviour, except those narrowly connected with religious rituals. 'Freedom of religion' becomes reduced to 'freedom of worship'.

Why should religious views be especially protected? All principles held conscientiously deserve respect. Religious understandings are, however, deeply rooted in human nature. The cognitive science of religion points to their ubiquity, and the way in which they are built into our basic cognitive architecture. That does not prove their truth, and such inchoate impulses can be expressed in many competing religious reactions. It does explain their tenacity, and their centrality in much human life. Religion is an integral part of what it is to be human.

Ignoring it as a component of human nature, and treating it as an idiosyncratic choice of no social significance, will underestimate its power and significance.

Religion is not just an individual matter. It flourishes in society. It has to be taught to children, and is characteristically expressed not only in public worship but in ways of life. Religious institutions will be necessary, and in many countries are bound up in various ways with the histories and traditions of those countries. Religion can flourish only when strong institutions influence its citizens and act as a buffer between them and a state that can become too fond of regulation. When the priorities of a democratic country appear to run counter to the policies of religious institutions, or the conscience of individuals, every effort should be made to accommodate both.

The strength of a democracy depends on its ability to make room for views and practices of which the majority may disapprove. Parliaments and courts can make a stand in favour of equality and non-discrimination, but in so doing run counter to religious consciences. Discrimination on the grounds of religion is still discrimination. Discounting religious principles in favour of the pursuit of equality fails to give equal weight to the consciences of some citizens. It still treats some citizens and their interests as more important than others. The pursuit of equality can itself produce a denial of that equality.

In the Republic of Ireland in 2010 there was a dispute about whether legislation allowing civil partnerships could allow for the inclusion of a freedom of religious conscience clause. Registrars faced criminal prosecution if they refused to conduct civil partnership ceremonies. Confronting the demand for exemptions for conscience, the Minister for Justice, Dermot Ahern, said in the *Dail* (the Irish lower house): 'It would run completely contrary to policy to allow public servants to pick and choose in respect of the view of either the *Oireachtas* (the Irish Parliament) or the Executive regarding duties which must be carried out…Anyone is entitled to know that the services in respect of which provision is made in legislation will be provided without fear or favour.'[9]

All public servants may have to administer laws of which they personally disapprove. That is the inevitable consequence of democracy. It is also essential for democracy that real sticking points of conscience, and especially objections arising from important religious beliefs, are respected. Legislatures, and courts, cannot escape recognizing, in particular instances, the substantial burden that laws may place on a religious conscience. This is of particular importance when the issue concerns an unpopular, or unfashionable, minority.

Irish laws are supposed to be subject to the Irish Constitution, and Article 44 says that 'freedom of conscience and the free profession and practice of religion are, subject to public order and morality, guaranteed to every citizen'.[10] The problem there, as in other countries, is that the state then imposes its own view of morality, which inevitably follows the fashions of the moment. No attempt is made at what has been termed 'reasonable accommodation'. Democratic agreement of public policy need not imply the enforcement of public norms, and a particular view of morality, on individuals. Doing so may be neater from a bureaucratic point of view, but it rides roughshod over the respect for individuals that should lie at the root of any democracy. It involves coercion, and introduces a new form of discrimination in policies designed to remove other forms.

The pursuit of equality can never produce a neutral viewpoint. We may change what we are prepared to tolerate, but public policy is always based on assumptions about what is important. At root, these judgements will themselves be implicitly philosophical, and even religious. If we believe human rights matter, and that all must be free and equal, we must have a conception of human nature, and why humans matter. In Western societies, these ideas have been bound up with Christian principles. The challenge of the twenty-first century is whether a strong conception of human dignity can survive long without the Christian roots that have undoubtedly nurtured it.

Notes

INTRODUCTION

1. See, e.g., Jan Narveson and James P. Sterba, *Are Liberty and Equality Compatible: For and Against* (Cambridge: Cambridge University Press, 2010).
2. Jeremy Waldron, *God, Locke and Equality: Christian Foundations in Locke's Political Thought* (Cambridge: Cambridge University Press, 2002), 2.
3. Richard Labunski, *James Madison and the Struggle for the Bill of Rights* (Oxford: Oxford University Press, 2006), 223.
4. This is a central theme of my *Religion in Public Life: Must Faith be Privatized* (Oxford: Oxford University Press, 2007).
5. See my *Religion in Public Life*, 116 ff.
6. Richard Moon, 'Sexual Orientation, Equality and Religious Freedom in the Public Schools', *Review of Constitutional Studies*, 8 (2003), 256.
7. Moon, 'Sexual Orientation, Equality and Religious Freedom in the Public Schools', 270.

CHAPTER I

1. See, e.g., J. Rawls, *The Law of Peoples* (Cambridge, MA: Harvard University Press, 1999), 127. I have written on Rawls's liberalism, particularly in connection with religion, elsewhere. See *Religion in Public Life: Must Faith be Privatized* (Oxford: Oxford University Press, 2007), 113 ff., 198 ff., *Morality Matters* (Oxford: Blackwell, 2002), 85 ff., and *Rationality and Religion: Does Faith Need Reason?* (Oxford: Blackwell, 1997), ch. 1.
2. For more on Kant's views on autonomy and their place in his philosophy, see my *Ideas of Human Nature* (2nd edn; Oxford: Blackwell, 1999), ch. 7.
3. A. C. Grayling, *Towards the Light* (London: Bloomsbury, 2007), 261.
4. Grayling, *Towards the Light*, 261.
5. Grayling, *Towards the Light*, 261.
6. See Trigg, *Morality Matters*, ch. 11.
7. W. F. Sullivan, *The Impossibility of Religious Freedom* (Princeton: Princeton University Press, 2005).
8. Sullivan, *The Impossibility of Religious Freedom*, 148.
9. Sullivan, *The Impossibility of Religious Freedom*, 152.
10. Sullivan, *The Impossibility of Religious Freedom*, 148.

11. Sullivan, *The Impossibility of Religious Freedom*, 150.

12. Sullivan, *The Impossibility of Religious Freedom*, 157.

13. Sullivan, *The Impossibility of Religious Freedom*, 157.

14. Grayling, *Towards the Light*, 131.

15. See A. J. Ayer, *Language, Truth and Logic* (2nd edn; London: Gollancz, 1946).

16. T. F. Farr, *World of Faith and Freedom* (New York: Oxford University Press, 2008), 47.

17. Farr, *World of Faith and Freedom*, 21.

18. A. Plantinga, *Warranted Christian Belief* (New York: Oxford University Press, 2000), 172.

19. J. L. Barrett, *Why Would Anyone Believe in God?* (Lanham, MD: Alta Mira Press 2004), 32.

20. Barrett, *Why Would Anyone Believe in God?*, 31.

21. P. Boyer, *Religion Explained* (London: Vintage, 2002), 187.

22. Barrett, *Why Would Anyone Believe in God?*, 78.

23. These were the responses of my granddaughter and grandson (twins aged 4) when faced with a similar task. At 3 they were sure their mother would know what had changed when she was out of the room. At 4 they were equally adamant that she would not know, but that God would.

24. J. L. Barrett, Rebekah A. Richert, and Amanda Driesenga, 'God's Beliefs versus Mother's: The Development of Nonhuman Agent Concepts', *Child Development*, 71 (2001), 6.

25. Barrett et al., 'God's Beliefs versus Mother's', 61.

26. Emma Cohen, *The Mind Possessed* (Oxford: Oxford University Press, 2007), 140.

27. Cohen, *The Mind Possessed*, 140.

28. P. Bloom, *Descartes' Baby* (London: Arrow Books, 2005), 203.

29. Bloom, *Descartes' Baby*, 207.

30. See, e.g., Dominic Johnson and Jesse Bering, 'Hand of God, Mind of Man: Punishment and Cognition', in Jeremy Schloss and Michael Murray (eds), *The Believing Primate* (Oxford: Oxford University Press, 2009), 39.

31. See Roger Trigg, *The Shaping of Man: Philosophical Aspects of Sociobiology* (Oxford: Blackwell, 1982).

32. Deborah Kelemen and Evelyn Rosset, 'The Human Function Component: Teleological Explanation in Adults', *Cognition*, 111 (2009), 138.

33. Kelemen and Rosset, 'The Human Function Component', 138.

34. Kelemen and Rosset, 'The Human Function Component', 138.

35. Kelemen and Rosset, 'The Human Function Component', 142.

36. Scott Atran, *In Gods We Trust* (New York: Oxford University Press, 2002), 280.

37. Barrett, *Why Would Anyone Believe in God?*, 91.

38. Barrett, *Why Would Anyone Believe in God?*, 91.

39. Johnson and Bering, 'Hand of God, Mind of Man', in Schloss and Murray (eds), *The Believing Primate*, 42.

40. Johnson and Bering, 'Hand of God', 41.

CHAPTER 2

1. See Roger Trigg, *Religion in Public Life: Must Faith be Privatized* (Oxford: Oxford University Press, 2007).
2. Thomas Jefferson Foundation, *Thomas Jefferson's Monticello* (Chapel Hill, NC: University of North Carolina Press, 2002), 87.
3. J. Waldron, *God, Locke and Equality: Christian Foundations in Locke's Political Thought* (Cambridge: Cambridge University Press, 2002), 82.
4. Taken from Thomas Jefferson, 'Notes on the State of Virginia', query XVIII, in Thomas Jefferson, *Writings* (New York: Library of America, 1984), 289.
5. Tage Kurten, 'The Christian Living in Two Worlds?' *Studia Theologica*, 61 (2007), 95.
6. Kurten, 'The Christian Living in Two Worlds?', 95.
7. Quoted in Inge Eidsvag, Tore Lindholm, and Barbro Sveen, 'The Emergence of Interfaith Dialogue: The Norwegian Experience', in Tore Lindholm, W. Cole Durham, and G. B. Tahzib-Lie (eds), *Facilitating Freedom of Religion or Belief: A Deskbook* (Leiden: Martinus Nijhoff, 2004), 778.
8. Martha C. Nussbaum, *Liberty of Conscience: In Defense of America's Tradition of Religious Equality* (New York: Basic Books, 2008), 2.
9. Nussbaum, *Liberty of Conscience*, 2.
10. See Trigg, *Religion in Public Life*, ch. 8, 'Under God?'.
11. Nussbaum, *Liberty of Conscience*, 21.
12. *Sanatan Dharma, Maha Sabha and Others* v. *The Attorney General of Trinidad and Tobago*, Judgment of the Lords of the Judicial Committee of the Privy Council, Appeal No. 53 of 2008, delivered 28 Apr. 2009, sect. 4.
13. *Sanatan Dharma, Maha Sabha and Others* v. *The Attorney General of Trinidad and Tobago*, sect. 3.
14. Ronald Dworkin, *Is Democracy Possible Here?* (Princeton: Princeton University Press, 2006), 61.
15. Dworkin, *Is Democracy Possible Here?*, 60.
16. Dworkin, *Is Democracy Possible Here?*, 61.
17. Dworkin, *Is Democracy Possible Here?*, 71.
18. Dworkin, *Is Democracy Possible Here?*, 71.
19. Dworkin, *Is Democracy Possible Here?*, 78.
20. Dworkin, *Is Democracy Possible Here?*, 70.
21. Dworkin, *Is Democracy Possible Here?*, 83.
22. For a contemporary argument, see Roger Trigg, *Rationality and Religion: Does Faith Need Reason?* (Oxford: Blackwell, 1997).
23. Dworkin, *Is Democracy Possible Here?*, 11.
24. Dworkin, *Is Democracy Possible Here?*, 9.
25. C. L. Eisgruber and L. G. Sager, *Religious Freedom and the Constitution* (Cambridge, MA: Harvard University Press, 2007), 19.
26. Eisgruber and Sager, *Religious Freedom and the Constitution*, 5.
27. Eisgruber and Sager, *Religious Freedom and the Constitution*, 52.

28. Eisgruber and Sager, *Religious Freedom and the Constitution*, 284.
29. Eisgruber and Sager, *Religious Freedom and the Constitution*, 5.
30. Eisgruber and Sager, *Religious Freedom and the Constitution*, 5.
31. *Moscow Branch of the Salvation Army* v. *Russia*, ECHR, Strasbourg, Application No. 72881/01, 5 Oct. 2006, para. 57.
32. *Moscow Branch of the Salvation Army* v. *Russia*, para. 57.
33. *Moscow Branch of the Salvation Army* v. *Russia*, para. 58.
34. *Moscow Branch of the Salvation Army* v. *Russia*, para. 58.
35. *Moscow Branch of the Salvation Army* v. *Russia*, para. 59.
36. Council of Europe, Parliamentary Assembly, *State, Religion, Secularity and Human Rights*, Recommendation 1804 (2007), para. 23.
37. Council of Europe, *State, Religion, Secularity and Human Rights*, para. 15.
38. Council of Europe, *State, Religion, Secularity and Human Rights*, para. 4.
39. Council of Europe, *State, Religion, Secularity and Human Rights*, para. 17.
40. Council of Europe, *State, Religion, Secularity and Human Rights*, para. 24.1.
41. Council of Europe, *State, Religion, Secularity and Human Rights*, para. 24.2.
42. D. Hoffman and J. Rowe QC, *Human Rights in the UK: An Introduction to the Human Rights Act 1998* (Harlow: Pearson Longman, 2003), app. 1 (setting out the Act), 302.

CHAPTER 3

1. *HJ (Iran) and HT (Cameroon)* v. *Secretary of State for the Home Department* (2010) UKSC 31, para. 11.
2. *HJ (Iran) and HT (Cameroon)* v. *Secretary of State for the Home Department*, para. 11.
3. *HJ (Iran) and HT (Cameroon)* v. *Secretary of State for the Home Department*, para. 11.
4. *HJ (Iran) and HT (Cameroon)* v. *Secretary of State for the Home Department*, para. 76.
5. See Roger Trigg, *Understanding Social Science* (2nd edn; Oxford: Blackwell, 2001), 201 ff.
6. *Syndicat Northcrest* v. *Amselem* (2004) 2 SCR (Canada), 576.
7. *Syndicat Northcrest* v. *Amselem* (2004) 2 SCR (Canada), 581.
8. *HJ (Iran) and HT (Cameroon)* v. *Secretary of State for the Home Department*, para. 2.
9. *HJ (Iran) and HT (Cameroon)* v. *Secretary of State for the Home Department*, para. 2.
10. See Thomas Alan Harvey, *Acquainted with Grief: Wang Mingdao's Stand for the Persecuted Church in China* (Grand Rapids, MI: Brazos Press, 2002).
11. Harvey, *Acquainted with Grief*, 168.
12. *Syndicat Northcrest* v. *Amselem*, 582.
13. Richard Moon, 'Introduction', in Richard Moon (ed.), *Law and Religious Pluralism in Canada* (Vancouver: UBC Press, 2008).
14. See, e.g., 'School Bans Sikh Boy from Wearing his Religious Dagger', *London Evening Standard*, 13 Oct. 2009.

15. *Multani* v. *CSBB* (2006) 1 SCR (Canada), 297.
16. *Multani* v. *CSBB*, J. Charron, 281.
17. See Lorraine E. Weinrib, 'Ontario's Sharia Law Debate: Ontario's Sharia Law Debate: Law and Politics under the *Charter*', in Moon (ed.), *Law and Religious Pluralism in Canada*, 239 ff.
18. See Roger Trigg,*Religion in Public Life: Must Faith be Privatized* (Oxford: Oxford University Press, 2007), 160 ff.
19. Weinrib, 'Ontario's Sharia Law Debate', 250.
20. Weinrib, 'Ontario's Sharia Law Debate', 250.
21. Weinrib, 'Ontario's Sharia Law Debate', 244.
22. Alfred Stepan, 'Religion, Democracy and the "Twin Tolerations"', *Journal of Democracy*, 11/4 (2000), 37.
23. Stepan, 'Religion, Democracy and the "Twin Tolerations"', 37.
24. *Christian Legal Society Chapter of the University California, Hastings College of the Law* v. *Martinez et al.*, 130 S. Cr. 2971, 2993.
25. *Christian Legal Society* v. *Martinez*, 130 S. Cr. at 3012 (2010).
26. *Christian Legal Society* v. *Martinez*, 130 S. Cr. at 3000.
27. *Bruker* v. *Marcovitz* (2007) 3 SCR (Canada), 3.
28. *Bruker* v. *Marcovitz* (2007) 3 SCR (Canada), 3.
29. *Bruker* v. *Marcovitz* (2007) 3 SCR (Canada), 637.
30. R. Moon, '*Bruker* v. *Mancouvitz*: "Divorce and the Marriage of Law and Religion"', *Supreme Court Law Review* (Canada), 42 (2008), 39.
31. *Bruker* v. *Marcovitz* (2007) 3 SCR (Canada), 656.
32. *Bruker* v. *Marcovitz* (2007) 3 SCR (Canada), 656.
33. *Bruker* v. *Marcovitz* (2007) 3 SCR (Canada), 656.
34. *Boy Scouts of America* v. *Dale*, 530 US 640 (2000).

CHAPTER 4

1. Erwin Chemerinsky, 'The Wren Cross Controversy: Religion and the Public University: Why Church and State Should Be Separate', *William and Mary Law Review*, 49 (2008), 2212.
2. Gerard V. Bradley, 'The Wren Cross Controversy: Religion at a Public University', *William and Mary Law Review*, 49 (2008), 2226.
3. Bradley, 'The Wren Cross Controversy', 2236.
4. See Roger Trigg, *Reason and Commitment* (Cambridge: Cambridge University Press, 1973), for a sustained discussion of relativism and religion.
5. See Roger Trigg, *Ideas of Human Nature* (2nd edn; Oxford Blackwell, 1999), ch. 10.
6. Bhikhu Parekh, *A New Politics of Identity* (Basingstoke: Palgrave Macmillan, 2008), 208.
7. Parekh, *A New Politics of Identity*, 208.
8. See, e.g., Roger Trigg, *Understanding Social Science* (2nd edn; Oxford: Blackwell, 2001), ch. 8.
9. Parekh, *A New Politics of Identity*, 225–6.

10. Parekh, *A New Politics of Identity*, 217.
11. Parekh, *A New Politics of Identity*, 217.
12. Parekh, *A New Politics of Identity*, 210.
13. Parekh, *A New Politics of Identity*, 210.
14. Parekh, *A New Politics of Identity*, 227.
15. Parekh, *A New Politics of Identity*, 227.
16. *Folgero and Others* v. *Norway*, ECHR, Application No. 15472/02, Judgment, Strasbourg 29 June 2007, para 9.
17. *Folgero and Others* v. *Norway*, para. 9.
18. *Folgero and Others* v. *Norway*, para. 9.
19. *Folgero and Others* v. *Norway*, para. 101.
20. *Folgero and Others* v. *Norway*, para. 84.
21. *Folgero and Others* v. *Norway*, para. 22.
22. *Folgero and Others* v. *Norway*, para. 95.
23. *Folgero and Others* v. *Norway*, Judgment, Joint Dissenting Opinion of Judges Wildhabere et al., 51.
24. *Folgero and Others* v. *Norway*, Joint Dissenting Opinion, 51.
25. *Folgero and Others* v. *Norway*, Joint Dissenting Opinion, 52.
26. *Folgero and Others* v. *Norway*, Joint Dissenting Opinion, 51.
27. *Folgero and Others* v. *Norway*, Joint Dissenting Opinion, 52.
28. *Folgero and Others* v. *Norway*, para. 85(f).
29. Tore Lindholm, 'Philosophical and Religious Justifications of Freedom of Religion or Belief', in Tore Lindholm, W. Cole Durham, and B. G. Tahzib Lie (eds), *Facilitating Freedom of Religion or Belief: A Deskbook* (Leiden: Martinus Nijhoff, 2004), 22.
30. Lindholm, 'Philosophical and Religious Justifications', 22.
31. Lindholm, 'Philosophical and Religious Justifications', 22.
32. Lindholm, 'Philosophical and Religious Justifications', 26.
33. Lindholm, 'Philosophical and Religious Justifications', 30.
34. Lindholm, 'Philosophical and Religious Justifications', 39.
35. See Tore Lindholm, 'The Tenacity of Identity Politics in Norway', in L. Christoffersen, Kjell A. Modeer, and Svend Andersen (eds), *Law and Religion in the 21st Century: Nordic Perspectives* (Copenhagen: Djof Publishing, 2010), 227.
36. Lindholm, 'The Tenacity of Identity Politics in Norway', 234.
37. Lindholm, 'The Tenacity of Identity Politics in Norway', 234.
38. Tariq Modood, *Multicultural Politics* (Edinburgh: Edinburgh University Press, 2005), 164.

CHAPTER 5

1. See Steve Pincus, *1688: The First Modern Revolution* (New Haven: Yale University Press 2009).
2. Pincus, *1688*, 12.

3. Pincus, *1688*, 433.

4. Paul Starr, *Freedom's Power: The True Force of Liberalism* (New York: Basic Books, 2007), 22.

5. Starr, *Freedom's Power*, 22.

6. Starr, *Freedom's Power*, 22.

7. Alan Dershowitz, *Blasphemy: How the Religious Right is Hijacking our Declaration of Independence* (Hoboken, NJ: John Wiley and Sons, 2007), 110.

8. Donald Marquand Dozer, *Portrait of a Free State: A History of Maryland* (Cambridge, MD: Tidewater Publishers, 1976), 143.

9. See W. W. Manross, *A History of the American Episcopal Church* (Milwaukee, WI: Morehouse, 1935).

10. John K. Nelson, *A Blessed Company: Parishes, Parsons and Parishioners in Anglican Virginia, 1690–1776* (Chapel Hill, NC: University of North Carolina Press, 2001), 43.

11. Nelson, *A Blessed Company*, 128.

12. Paula S. Felder, *Forgotten Companions: The First Settlers of Spotsylvania County and Fredericksburgh Town* (2nd edn; Fredericksburg, VA: American History Company, 2000), 54.

13. Felder, *Forgotten Companions*, 54.

14. Jeff Broadwater, *George Mason, Forgotten Founder* (Chapel Hill, NC: University of North Carolina Press, 2006), 82.

15. Broadwater, *George Mason*, 85.

16. Chris Beneke, *Beyond Toleration* (New York: Oxford University Press, 2006), 136.

17. State of Virginia, *The Bill of Rights and the Constitution of the Commonwealth of Virginia*, 29 June 1776 (Hinesville, GA: Nova Anglia, Historical Reproductions).

18. *The Virginia Statute for Religious Freedom*, ed. Merrill D. Peterson and Robert C. Vaughan (Cambridge: Cambridge University Press, 1988), p. xvii.

19. *The Virginia Statute for Religious Freedom*, p. xvii.

20. *The Virginia Statute for Religious Freedom*, p. xviii.

21. Thomas Jefferson, 'Notes on the State of Virginia', in Thomas Jefferson, *Writings* (New York: Library of America, 1984), 285.

22. Forest Church's comment introducing the statute, in Forest Church (ed.), *The Separation of Church and State* (Boston: Beacon Press, 2004), 72.

23. Jefferson, 'Notes on the State of Virginia', 286.

24. James Madison, in Clinton Rossiter (ed.), *The Federalist Papers* (New York: Signet, 2003), no. 51, p. 321.

25. Jefferson, 'Notes on the State of Virginia', 283.

26. Nelson, *A Blessed Company*, 7.

27. James Madison, *Memorial and Remonstrance against Religious Assessments*, in Church (ed.), *The Separation of Church and State*, 67.

28. Madison, *Memorial and Remonstrance*, 67.

29. Madison, *Memorial and Remonstrance*, 63.

30. Madison, *Memorial and Remonstrance*, 63.
31. Madison, *Memorial and Remonstrance*, 64.
32. Madison, *Memorial and Remonstrance*, 64.
33. Martha C. Nussbaum, *Liberty of Conscience: In Defense of America's Tradition of Religious Equality* (New York: Basic Books, 2008), 95.
34. Nussbaum, *Liberty of* Conscience, 225.
35. *Aston Cantlow and Wilmcote with Billesley Parochial Church Council* v. *Wallbank* (2003) UKHL 37, per Lord Nicholls of Birkenhead, para. 13.
36. *Aston Cantlow et al.* v. *Wallbank*, para 13.
37. *Aston Cantlow et al.* v. *Wallbank*, per Lord Hope, para. 61.
38. *Lautsi v. Italy*, ECHR, Strasbourg, 3 Nov. 2009 (30814/06), para. 56.
39. *Lautsi v. Italy*, ECHR, Strasbourg, Grand Chamber, 18 Mar. 2011 (30814/06), para. 68.
40. *Lautsi v. Italy*, ECHR, Strasbourg, Grand Chamber, 18 Mar. 2011, para. 74.
41. *Lautsi v. Italy*, ECHR, Strasbourg, Grand Chamber, 18 Mar. 2011, Concurring Judgment by Judge Bonello, para. 1.2.
42. *Lautsi v. Italy*, ECHR, Strasbourg, Grand Chamber, 18 Mar. 2011, Bonello, para. 1.5.
43. *Lautsi v. Italy*, ECHR, Strasbourg, Grand Chamber, 18 Mar. 2011, Bonello, para. 36.
44. *Lautsi v. Italy*, ECHR, Strasbourg, Grand Chamber, 18 Mar. 2011, Judgment, para. 11.6.

CHAPTER 6

1. Charles Taylor, *A Secular Age* (Cambridge, MA: Belknap Harvard, 2007), 61.
2. Taylor, *A Secular Age*, 21.
3. See Roger Trigg, *Morality Matters* (Oxford: Blackwell, 2005), ch. 3
4. James Madison, *Memorial and Remonstrance against Religious Assessments*, in Forrest Church (ed.), *The Separation of Church and State* (Boston: Beacon Press), 61.
5. Madison, *Memorial and Remonstrance*, 62.
6. See Jeff Broadwater, *George Mason: Forgotten Founder* (Chapel Hill, NC: University of North Carolina Press, 2006), 147.
7. Madison, *Memorial and Remonstrance*, 62.
8. Philip Hamburger, 'More is Less', *Virginia Law Review*, 90 (2004), 835.
9. Hamburger, 'More is Less', 836.
10. See them chronicled in Vincent Munoz, *God and the Founders: Madison, Washington and Jefferson* (Cambridge: Cambridge University Press, 2009).
11. Philip Hamburger, 'Religious Freedom in Philadelphia', *Emory Law Journal*, 54 (2005), 1606.
12. Hamburger, 'Religious Freedom in Philadelphia', 1630.
13. Hamburger, 'More is Less', 837.
14. *Ladele v. London Borough of Islington* (2009) EWCA Civ. 1357 (15 Dec. 2009).
15. *Ladele v. London Borough of Islington*, para. 28.

16. *Ladele* v. *London Borough of Islington*, para. 51.
17. *Ladele* v.*London Borough of Islington*, para. 51.
18. *Ladele* v. *London Borough of Islington*, para. 52.
19. *Ladele* v. *London Borough of Islington*, para. 56.
20. See Roger Trigg, *Reason and Commitment* (Cambridge: Cambridge University Press, 1973), for a discussion about the respective roles of propositional belief and wider commitment in religion.
21. Ephesians 5: 25.

CHAPTER 7

1. State of Victoria, *Charter of Rights and Responsibilities Act 2006*, no. 43/2006.
2. State of Victoria, *Charter of Rights and Responsibilities*, 14.
3. *Lina Joy* v. *Majilis Ayama Islam Wilayah Persekutuan & 2 Lagi*, Malyasian Federal Court, No. 01–2–2006 (Judgment 30 May 2007).
4. State of Victoria, *Charter of Rights and Responsibilities*, 7(2).
5. John Locke, *A Letter Concerning Toleration*, in Locke, *Two Treatises of Government and A Letter Concerning Toleration*, ed. Ian Shapiro (New Haven: Yale University Press, 2003), 232.
6. Locke, *A Letter Concerning Toleration*, 233.
7. Locke, *A Letter Concerning Toleration*, 220.
8. Locke, *A Letter Concerning Toleration*, 243.
9. Locke, *A Letter Concerning Toleration*, 239.
10. Jean Bethke Elshtain, *Sovereignty, God and Self* (New York: Basic Books, 2008), 128.
11. Vaclav Havel, *Living in Truth*, trans Jan Vladislav (London: Faber and Faber 1986), 45 (significantly quoted with reference to China in T. A. Harvey, *Acquainted with Grief: Wang Mingdao's Stand for the Persecuted Church in China* (Grand Rapids, MI: Brazos Press, 2002), 103).
12. See Roger Trigg, *Reason and Commitment* (Cambridge: Cambridge University Press, 1973).
13. *Syndicat Northcrest v. Amselem* (2004) 2 SCR (Canada), 581.
14. *Syndicat Northcrest v. Amselem*, 581.
15. *Syndicat Northcrest v. Amselem*, 576.
16. *Syndicat Northcrest v. Amselem*, 581.
17. *Syndicat Northcrest v. Amselem*, 577.
18. *Syndicat Northcrest v. Amselem*, Justice Bastarache, dissenting, 625.
19. *Syndicat Northcrest v. Amselem*, Justice Bastarache, dissenting, 613.
20. *Syndicat Northcrest v. Amselem*, Justice Bastarache, dissenting, 613.
21. J. Savulescu, 'Two Worlds Apart: Religion and Ethics', *Journal of Medical Ethics*, 24 (1998), 383.
22. Savulescu, 'Two Worlds Apart', 383.
23. See Roger Trigg, *Rationality and Religion: Does Faith Need Reason?* (Oxford: Blackwell, 1998).
24. See Roger Trigg, *Morality Matters* (Oxford: Blackwell, 2005).

25. J. Savulescu, 'Conscientious Objection in Medicine', *British Medical Journal*, 332 (2006), 297.
26. Savulescu, 'Conscientious Objection in Medicine', 294.
27. Savulescu, 'Conscientious Objection in Medicine', 295.
28. Savulescu, 'Conscientious Objection in Medicine', 295.
29. Savulescu, 'Conscientious Objection in Medicine', 295.

CHAPTER 8

1. See Alexander Bonnici, *Medieval and Roman Inquisition in Malta* (Rabat, Malta: RUH, 1998).
2. *Employment Division, Department of Human Resources of Oregon v. Smith*, 494 US 872 (1990).
3. *Employment Division* v. *Smith*, 882.
4. *Employment Division* v. *Smith*, 888.
5. Kent Greenawalt, *Religion and the Constitution: Free Exercise and Fairness* (Princeton: Princeton University Press, 2006), i. 78.
6. *Employment Division* v. *Smith*, 890.
7. Quoted in Winnifred Fallers Sullivan, *The Impossibility of Religious Freedom* (Princeton: Princeton University Press, 2005), 22.
8. Greenawalt, *Religion and the Constitution*, 201.
9. See Roger Trigg, *Religion in Public Life: Must Faith be Privatized?* (Oxford: Oxford University Press, 2007), 157 ff.
10. See Trigg, *Religion in Public Life*, 158.
11. Greenawalt, *Religion and the Constitution*, 205.
12. Greenawalt, *Religion and the Constitution*, 205.
13. *R.* v. *JFS* (2009) UKSC 15, 16 Dec. 2009, para. 103.
14. *R.* v. *JFS*, para. 69.
15. *R.* v. *JFS*, para. 70.
16. *R.* v. *JFS*, para. 119.
17. *R.* v. *JFS*, para. 157.
18. *R.* v. *JFS*, para. 157.
19. *R.* v. *JFS*, para. 229.
20. *R.* v. *JFS*, para. 225.
21. *R.* v. *JFS*, para. 226.
22. *R.* v. *JFS*, para. 69.
23. *Catholic Care and the Charity Commission for England and Wales and the Equality and Human Rights Commission* (2010) EWHC 520 (Ch), para. 107.
24. *Catholic Care and the Charity Commission*, para. 105.
25. *Catholic Care and the Charity Commission*, para. 105.
26. *Catholic Care and the Charity Commission*, para. 106.
27. See *Schuth* v. *Germany*, ECHR 1620/03, 23 Sept. 2010, para. 72.
28. *Schuth* v. *Germany*, para. 70.
29. Alvin Esau, 'Living by Different Law', in Richard Moon (ed.), *Law and Religious Pluralism in Canada* (Vancouver: UBC Press, 2008), 128.

30. Esau, 'Living by Different Law', 129.
31. *Percy v. Church of Scotland Board of National Mission* (2005) UKHL 73.
32. *Percy v. Church of Scotland*, para. 34.
33. *Percy v. Church of Scotland*, para. 34.
34. R. M. Morris (ed.), *Church and State in 21st Century Britain: The Future of Church Establishment* (Basingstoke: Palgrave Macmillan, 2009), 98.
35. Morris (ed.), *Church and State in 21st Century Britain*, 78.
36. For an account of this history, see Lord Rodger of Earlsferry, *The Courts, the Church and the Constitution: Aspects of the Disruption of 1843* (Edinburgh: Edinburgh University Press, 2008).
37. Lord Rodger of Earlsferry, *The Courts, the Church and the Constitution*, 112.
38. Lord Rodger of Earlsferry, *The Courts, the Church and the Constitution*, 93.
39. Martha C. Nussbaum, *Liberty of Conscience: In Defense of America's Tradition of Religious Equality* (New York: Basic Books, 2008), 197.
40. See Roger Trigg, *Morality Matters* (Oxford: Blackwell, 2005), esp. ch. 2.
41. See Gerard Bouchard and Charles Taylor, *Building the Future: Abridged Report* (Quebec: Consultation Commission on Accommodation Practices Related to Cultural Differences, Government of Quebec, 2008), 23.
42. Bouchard and Taylor, *Building the Future*, 23.
43. Bouchard and Taylor, *Building the Future*, 25.
44. Bouchard and Taylor, *Building the Future*, 25.
45. Bouchard and Taylor, *Building the Future*, 25.
46. Bouchard and Taylor, *Building the Future*, 26.
47. Bouchard and Taylor, *Building the Future*, 45.
48. Bouchard and Taylor, *Building the Future*, 49.

CHAPTER 9

1. Tom Bingham, *The Rule of Law* (London: Allen Lane, 2010), 55.
2. Bingham, *The Rule of Law*, 57.
3. John Locke, 'A Letter Concerning Toleration' in Locke, *Two Treatises of Government and A Letter Concerning Toleration*, ed. Ian Shapiro (New Haven: Yale University Press, 2003), 245.
4. See Steve Pincus, *1688: The First Modern Revolution* (New Haven: Yale University Press, 2009), 178.
5. Gerard Bouchard and Charles Taylor, *Building the Future: Abridged Report* (Quebec: Consultation Commission on Accommodation Practices Related to Cultural Differences, Government of Quebec, 2008), 28.
6. *Alberta v. Hutterian Brethren of Wilson Colony* (2009) 2 SCR (Canada), 567.
7. *Alberta v. Hutterian Brethren of Wilson Colony*, Justice LeBel, para. 201.
8. *Alberta v. Hutterian Brethren of Wilson Colony*, Chief Justice Mclachlin, para. 90.
9. *Eweida v. British Airways* (2010) EWCA Civ. 80, para. 6.
10. *Eweida v. British Airways*, para. 8.
11. *Eweida v. British Airways*, para. 40.

12. *R (Eunice Johns and Owen Johns) and Derby City Council and Equality and Human Rights Commission* (2011) EWHC 375 (Admin), para. 99.

13. *Alberta v. Hutterian Brethren* (2009), para. 69.

14. Tore Lindholm, 'Philosophical and Religious Justifications of Freedom of Religion or Belief', in T. Lindholm, et al. (eds), *Facilitating Freedom of Religion or Belief: A Deskbook* (Leiden: Martinus Nijhoff, 2004), 47.

15. Johan D. van der Vyer, 'The Relationship of Freedom of Religion or Belief Norms to Other Human Rights', in Lindholm et al. (eds), *Facilitating Freedom of Religion or Belief: A Deskbook*, 114.

16. Van der Vyer, 'The Relationship of Freedom', 119.

17. Van der Vyer, 'The Relationship of Freedom', 120.

18. Bingham, *The Rule of Law*, 79.

19. Jeremy Waldron, *God, Locke and Equality: Christian Foundations in Locke's Political Thought* (Cambridge: Cambridge University Press, 2002), 227.

20. Richard Dawkins, *The God Delusion* (London: Bantam Press, 2006), 317.

21. Dawkins, *The God Delusion*, 339.

22. Dawkins, *The God Delusion*, 340.

23. Dawkins, *The God Delusion*, 340.

24. See Roger Trigg, *Morality Matters* (Oxford: Blackwell, 2005), 85 ff.

25. Matthew Clayton, *Justice and Legitimacy in Upbringing* (Oxford: Oxford University Press, 2006), 93.

26. Clayton, *Justice and Legitimacy*, 120.

CHAPTER 10

1. Alexis de Tocqueville, *Democracy in America* (New York: Bantam, 2002), i. 355.

2. Tocqueville, *Democracy in America*, i. 355.

3. Tocqueville, *Democracy in America*, i. 357.

4. Tocqueville, *Democracy in America*, i. 359.

5. See Vincent Phillip Munoz, *God and the Founders: Madison, Washington and Jefferson* (Cambridge: Cambridge University Press, 2009).

6. Thomas Jefferson, 'Notes on the State of Virginia', query XVII, in Thomas Jefferson, *Writings* (New York: Library of America, 1984), 285.

7. See Roger Trigg, *Rationality and Science* (Oxford: Blackwell, 1993).

8. Alfred Stepan, 'Religion, Democracy and the "Twin Tolerations"', *Journal of Democracy*, 11/4 (2000), 44.

9. See Roger Trigg, *Understanding Social Science* (2nd edn; Oxford: Blackwell, 2001), 126 ff., for a further discussion of this in the context of a social science.

10. See Roger Trigg, *Reality at Risk: A Defence of Realism in Philosophy and the Sciences* (2nd edn; Hemel Hempstead: Harvester Wheatsheaf (Simon and Shuster), 1989), 134 ff.

11. *Washington Post*, 8 May 2010.

12. *McFarlane v. Relate Avon Ltd* (2010) EWCA Civ. B1 (29 Apr. 2010), para. 21.

13. *McFarlane* v. *Relate Avon Ltd*, para. 22.
14. *McFarlane* v. *Relate Avon Ltd*, para. 24.
15. *McFarlane* v. *Relate Avon Ltd*, para. 23.
16. *McFarlane* v. *Relate Avon Ltd*, para. 23.
17. *McFarlane* v. *Relate Avon Ltd*, para. 23.
18. *McFarlane* v. *Relate Avon Ltd*, para. 24.
19. For arguments to the contrary, see Roger Trigg, *Reason and Commitment* (Cambridge: Cambridge University Press, 1973), and *Rationality and Religion: Does Faith Need Reason?* (Oxford: Blackwell, 1998). See also Roger Trigg, *Religion in Public Life: Must Faith be Privatized?* (Oxford: Oxford University Press, 2007).
20. *McFarlane* v. *Relate Avon Ltd*, para. 24.
21. *McFarlane* v. *Relate Avon Ltd*, para. 25.
22. *McFarlane* v. *Relate Avon Ltd*, para. 25.
23. *Salazar v. Buono*, 130 S. Cr. 1803 (2010).
24. *McFarlane* v. *Relate Avon Ltd*, para. 24.
25. Nicholas Wolterstorff, *Justice: Rights and Wrongs* (Princeton: Princeton University Press, 2008), 360.
26. Wolterstorff, *Justice*, 360.
27. Nicholas Wolterstorff, 'How Social Justice Got to me and why it Never Left', *Journal of the American Academy of Religion*, 76 (2008), 673.
28. See Roger Trigg. *Ideas of Human Nature* (2nd edn; Oxford: Blackwell, 1999), for different approaches to this.
29. Martha C. Nussbaum, *Liberty of Conscience: In Defense of America's Tradition of Religious Equality* (New York: Basic Books, 2008), 226.
30. Nussbaum, *Liberty of Conscience*, 226.
31. Nussbaum, *Liberty of Conscience*, 226.
32. James Griffin, *On Human Rights* (Oxford: Oxford University Press 2008), 21.
33. Griffin, *On Human Rights*, 45.
34. Griffin, *On Human Rights*, 50.
35. Griffin, *On Human Rights*, 26.
36. For more on Nietzsche, see Roger Trigg, *Ideas of Human Nature* (2nd edn; Oxford: Blackwell, 1999), ch. 10, pp. 139 ff.
37. Trigg, *Ideas of Human Nature*, 150.
38. See Roger Trigg, *Philosophy Matters* (Oxford: Blackwell, 2002), for a discussion of postmodernism and relativism.

CONCLUSION

1. Thomas Jefferson, 'Bill for Establishing Religious Freedom', in Thomas Jefferson, *Writings* (New York: Library of America, 1984), 346.
2. *R (Eunice Johns and Owen Johns) and Derby City Council and Equality and Human Rights Commission* (2011) EWCH 375 (Admin), para. 36.
3. *R (Eunice Johns and Owen Johns) and Derby City Council*, para. 39.
4. *R (Eunice Johns and Owen Johns) and Derby City Council*, para. 38.

5. *R (Eunice Johns and Owen Johns) and Derby City Council*, para. 39.
6. See C. Taliaferro and A. J. Teply (eds), *Cambridge Platonist Spirituality* (New York: Paulist Press, 2004).
7. See 'Foster Parents Defeated by New Inquisition', *Daily Telegraph*, Editorial, 1 Mar. 2011.
8. Alexander Bonnici, *Medieval and Roman Inquisition in Malta* (Rabat, Malta: RUH, 1998), 177.
9. *Dail Eireann*, second stage of Civil Partnership Bill, 27 Jan. 2010.
10. *Constitution of Ireland (Bunreacht na hÉireann)* (Dublin: Government Publications, first enacted 1937).

Bibliography

LEGAL REFERENCES

Alberta v. *Hutterian Brethren of Wilson Colony* 2009 SCC (Canada), 37.

Aston Cantlow and Wilmcote with Billesley Parochial Church Council v. *Wallbank* (2003) UKHL 37.

Boy Scouts of America v. *Dale*, 530 US 640 (2000).

Bruker v. *Marcovitz* 2007 SCC 54 (Canada).

Catholic Care and the Charity Commission for England and Wales and the Equality and Human Rights Commission (2010) EWHC 520 (Ch).

Christian Legal Society Chapter of the University California, Hastings College of the Law v. *Martinez et al.*, 130 S. Cr. 2971 (2010).

Employment Division, Department of Human Resources of Oregon v. *Smith*, 494 US 872 (1990).

Eweida v. *British Airways* (2010) EWCA Civ. 80.

Folgero and Others v. *Norway*, ECHR, Application No. 15472/02, Judgment, Strasbourg, 29 June 2007.

HJ (Iran) and HT (Cameroon) v. *Secretary of State for the Home Department* (2010) UKSC 31.

Ladele v. *London Borough of Islington* (2009) EWCA Civ. 1357 (15 Dec. 2009).

Lautsi v. *Italy*, ECHR, Strasbourg, 3 Nov. 2009 (30814/06).

Lautsi v. *Italy*, ECHR, Strasbourg, Grand Chamber, 18 Mar. 2010 (30814/06).

Lina Joy v. *Majilis Ayama Islam Wilayah Persekutuan & 2 Lagi*, Malaysian Federal Court, no. 01–2–2006 (Judgment 30 May 2007).

McFarlane v. *Relate Avon Ltd* (2010) EWCA Civ. B1.

Moscow Branch of the Salvation Army v. *Russia*, ECHR, Strasbourg, Application No. 72881/01, 5 Oct. 2006.

Multani v. *CSSB* 2006 SCC 6 (Canada).

Percy v. *Church of Scotland Board of National Mission* (2005) UKHL 73.

R. v. *JFS* (2009) UKSC 15.

R (Eunice Johns and Owen Johns) and Derby City Council and Equality and Human Rights Commission (2011) EWCH 375 (Admin).

Salazar v. *Buono*, 130 S. Cr. 1803 (2010).

Sanatan Dharma, Maha Sabha and Others v. *The Attorney General of Trinidad and Tobago*, Judgment of the Lords of the Judicial Committee of the Privy Council, Appeal No. 53 of 2008, delivered 28 Apr. 2009.

Schuth v. *Germany*, ECHR 1620/03, 23 Sept. 2010.
Syndicat Northcrest v. *Amselem* 2004 SCC 47 (Canada), 47.

OTHER REFERENCES

Atran, S., *In Gods We Trust* (New York: Oxford University Press, 2002).

Ayer, A. J., *Language, Truth and Logic* (2nd edn; London: Gollancz, 1946).

Barrett, J. L., *Why Would Anyone Believe in God?* (Lanham, MD: Alta Mira Press, 2004).

Barrett, J. L., Richert, R. A., and Driesanga, A., 'God's Beliefs versus Mother's: The Development of Nonhuman Agent Concepts', *Child Development*, 71 (2001).

Beneke, C., *Beyond Toleration* (New York: Oxford University Press, 2006).

Bingham, T., *The Rule of Law* (London: Allen Lane, 2010).

Bloom, P., *Descartes' Baby* (London: Arrow Books, 2005)

Bonnici, A., *Medieval and Roman Inquisition in Malta* (Rabat, Malta: RUH, 1998).

Bouchard, G., and Taylor, C., *Building the Future: Abridged Report* (Quebec: Consultation Commission on Accommodation Practices Related to Cultural Differences, Government of Quebec, 2008).

Boyer, P., *Religion Explained* (London: Vintage, 2002).

Bradley, G.V., 'The Wren Cross Controversy: Religion at a Public University', *William and Mary Law Review*, 49 (2008).

Broadwater J., *George Mason, Forgotten Founder* (Chapel Hill, NC: University of North Carolina Press, 2006).

Chemerinsky, E., 'The Wren Cross Controversy: Religion and the Public University: Why Church and State Should Be Separate', *William and Mary Law Review*, 49 (2008).

Christoffersen, L., Modeer, K. A., and Andersen, S., *Law and Religion in the 21st Century: Nordic Perspectives* (Copenhagen: Djof, 2010).

Church, F. (ed.), *The Separation of Church and State* (Boston: Beacon Press, 2004).

Clayton, M., *Justice and Legitimacy in Upbringing* (Oxford: Oxford University Press, 2006).

Cohen, E., *The Mind Possessed* (Oxford: Oxford University Press, 2007).

Constitution of Ireland (Bunreacht na hÉireann) (Dublin: Government Publications, first enacted 1937).

Council of Europe, Parliamentary Assembly, *State, Religion, Secularity and Human Rights*, Rec, 1804 (2007).

Dawkins, R., *The God Delusion* (London: Bantam Press, 2006).

Dershowitz, A., *Blasphemy: How the Religious Right is Hijacking our Declaration of Independence* (Hoboken, NJ: John Wiley and Sons, 2007).

Dozer, D. M., *Portrait of a Free State: A History of Maryland* (Cambridge, MD: Tidewater Publishers, 1976).

Dworkin, R., *Is Democracy Possible Here?* (Princeton: Princeton University Press, 2006).

Eisgruber, C. L., and Sager, L. G., *Religious Freedom and the Constitution* (Cambridge, MA: Harvard University Press, 2007).

Elshtain, Jean Bethke, *Sovereignty, God and Self* (New York: Basic Books, 2008).

Esau, A., 'Living by Different Law', in Richard Moon (ed.), *Law and Religious Pluralism in Canada* (Vancouver: UBC Press, 2008).

Farr, T. F., *World of Faith and Freedom* (New York: Oxford University Press, 2008).

Felder P. S., *Forgotten Companions: The First Settlers of Spotsylvania County and Fredericksburgh Town* (2nd edn; Fredericksburg, VA: American History Company, 2000).

Grayling, A. C., *Towards the Light* (London: Bloomsbury, 2007).

Greenawalt, K., *Religion and the Constitution: Volume 1, Free Exercise and Fairness* (Princeton: Princeton University Press, 2006).

Griffin, J., *On Human Rights* (Oxford: Oxford University Press, 2008).

Harvey, T. A., *Acquainted with Grief: Wang Mingdao's Stand for the Persecuted Church in China* (Grand Rapids, MI: Brazos Press, 2002).

Havel, V., *Living in Truth*, trans. J. Vladislav (London: Faber and Faber, 1986).

Hamburger, P., 'More is Less', *Virginia Law Review*, 90 (2004).

Hamburger, P., 'Religious Freedom in Philadelphia', *Emory Law Journal*, 54 (2005).

Hill, M., *Ecclesiastical Law* (3rd edn; Oxford: Oxford University Press, 2007).

Hoffman, D., and Rowe, J., QC, *Human Rights in the UK: An Introduction to the Human Rights Act 1998* (Harlow: Pearson Longman, 2003).

Jefferson, T., *Writings* (New York: Library of America, 1984).

Johnson, D., and Bering, J., 'Hand of God, Mind of Man: Punishment and Cognition', in Jeremy Schloss and Michael Murray (eds), *The Believing Primate* (Oxford: Oxford University Press, 2009).

Keleman, D., and Rosset, E., 'The Human Function Component: Teleological Explanation in Adults', *Cognition*, 111 (2009).

Kurten, T., 'The Christian Living in Two Worlds', *Studia theologica*, 61 (2007).

Labunski, R., *James Madison and the Struggle for the Bill of Rights* (Oxford: Oxford University Press, 2006).

Lindholm, T., 'Philosophical and Religious Justifications of Freedom of Religion or Belief', in T. Lindholm, W. Cole Durham, and B. G. Tahzib-Lie (eds), *Facilitating Freedom of Religion or Belief: A Deskbook* (Leiden: Martinus Nijhoff, 2004).

Lindholm, T., 'The Tenacity of Identity Politics in Norway', in L. Christoffersen, Kjell A. Modeer, and Svend Andersen (eds), *Law and Religion in the 21st Century: Nordic Perspectives* (Copenhagen: Djof Publishing, 2010).

Lindholm, T., Durham W., Cole, and Tahzib Lie, B. G. (eds), *Facilitating Freedom of Religion or Belief: A Deskbook* (Leiden: Martinus Nijhoff, 2004).

Locke, J., *Two Treatises of Government and A Letter Concerning Toleration* (New Haven: Yale University Press, 2003).

Madison, James, *Memorial and Remonstrance against Religious Assessments*, in Forrest Church (ed.), *The Separation of Church and State* (Boston: Beacon Press).

Manross, W. W., *A History of the American Episcopal Church* (Milwaukee, WI: Morehouse, 1935).

Modood, T., *Multicultural Politics* (Edinburgh: Edinburgh University Press, 2005).

Moon R., 'Sexual Orientation, Equality and Religious Freedom in the Public Schools', *Review of Constitutional Studies*, 8 (2003).

Moon R., '*Bruker v. Marcowitz*: "Divorce and the Marriage of Law and Religion"', *Supreme Court Law Review* (Canada), 42 (2008).

Moon, R. (ed.), *Law and Religious Pluralism in Canada* (Vancouver: UBC Press, 2008).

Morris, R. M. (ed.), *Church and State in 21st Century Britain: The Future of Church Establishment* (Basingstoke: Palgrave Macmillan, 2009).

Munoz, V. P., *God and the Founders: Madison, Washington and Jefferson* (Cambridge: Cambridge University Press, 2009).

Narveson, J., and Sterba, J. P., *Are Liberty and Equality Compatible? For and Against* (Cambridge: Cambridge University Press, 2010).

Nelson, J. K., *A Blessed Company: Parishes, Parsons and Parishioners in Anglican Virginia, 1690–1776* (Chapel Hill, NC: University of North Carolina Press, 2001).

Nussbaum, M. C., *Liberty of Conscience: In Defense of America's Tradition of Religious Equality* (New York: Basic Books, 2008).

Parekh, Bhikhu, *A New Politics of Identity* (Basingstoke: Palgrave Macmillan, 2008).

Peterson, M. D., and Vaughan, R. C. 'Preface', in *The Virginia Statute for Religious Freedom*, ed. M. D. Peterson and R. C. Vaughan (Cambridge: Cambridge University Press, 1988).

Pincus, S., *1688: The First Modern Revolution* (New Haven: Yale University Press, 2009).

Plantinga, A., *Warranted Christian Belief* (New York: Oxford University Press, 2000).

Rawls, J., *The Law of Peoples* (Cambridge, MA: Harvard University Press, 1999).

Rodger of Earlsferrry, Lord, *The Courts, the Church and the Constitution: Aspects of the Disruption of 1843* (Edinburgh: Edinburgh University Press, 2008).

Rossiter, C. (ed.), *The Federalist Papers* (New York: Signet, 2003).

Savulescu, J., 'Two Worlds Apart: Religion and Ethics', *Journal of Medical Ethics*, 24 (1998).

Savulescu, J., 'Conscientious Objection in Medicine', *British Medical Journal*, 332 (2006).

Schloss, J., and Murray, M. (eds), *The Believing Primate* (Oxford: Oxford University Press, 2009).

Starr, P., *Freedom's Power: The True Force of Liberalism* (New York: Basic Books, 2007).

State of Victoria, *Charter of Rights and Responsibilities Act 2006*, no. 43/2006.

State Of Virginia, *The Bill of Rights and the Constitution of the Commonwealth of Virginia*, 29 June 1776 (Hinesville, GA: Nova Anglia Company, Historical Reproductions).

Stepan, A., 'Religion, Democracy, and the "Twin Tolerations"', *Journal of Democracy*, 11/4 (2000).

Sullivan, W. F., *The Impossibility of Religious Freedom* (Princeton: Princeton University Press, 2005).

Taylor C., *A Secular Age* (Cambridge, MA: Belknap, Harvard University Press, 2007).

Thomas Jefferson Foundation, *Thomas Jefferson's Monticello* (Chapel Hill, NC: University of North Carolina Press, 2002).

Tocqueville, de, Alexis, *Democracy in America* (New York: Bantam, 2002).

Trigg, R., *Reason and Commitment* (Cambridge: Cambridge University Press, 1973).

Trigg, R., *The Shaping of Man: Philosophical Aspects of Sociobiology* (Oxford: Blackwell, 1982).

Trigg, R., *Reality at Risk: A Defence of Realism in Philosophy and the Sciences* (2nd edn; Hemel Hempstead: Harvester Wheatsheaf (Simon and Schuster), 1989).

Trigg, R., *Rationality and Science* (Oxford: Blackwell, 1993).

Trigg, R., *Rationality and Religion: Does Faith Need Reason?* (Oxford: Blackwell, 1998).

Trigg, R., *Ideas of Human Nature* (2nd edn; Oxford: Blackwell, 1999).

Trigg, R., *Understanding Social Science* (2nd edn; Oxford: Blackwell, 2001).

Trigg, R., *Philosophy Matters* (Oxford: Blackwell, 2002).

Trigg, R., *Morality Matters* (Oxford: Blackwell, 2005).

Trigg, R., *Religion in Public Life: Must Faith be Privatized?* (Oxford: Oxford University Press, 2007).

Trigg, R., *Free To Believe? Religious Freedom in a Liberal Society* (London: Theos Think Tank, 2010).

Van der Vyer, J. D., 'The Relationship of Freedom of Religion or Belief Norms to Other Human Rights', in T. Lindholm, W. Cole Durham, and B. G. Tahzib-Lie (eds), *Facilitating Freedom of Religion or Belief: A Deskbook* (Leiden: Martinus Nijhoff, 2004).

The Virginia Statute for Religious Freedom, ed. M. D. Peterson and R. C. Vaughan (Cambridge: Cambridge University Press, 1988).

Waldron, J., *God, Locke and Equality: Christian Foundations in Locke's Political Thought* (Cambridge: Cambridge University Press, 2002).

Wolterstorff, N., 'How Social Justice Got to me and why it Never Left', *Journal of the American Academy of Religion*, 76 (2008).

Wolterstorff, N., *Justice: Rights and Wrongs* (Princeton: Princeton University Press, 2008).

Index